SLAVERY IN AMERICAN HISTORY

THE SLAVE TRADE IN AMERICA

CRUEL COMMERCE

RICHARD WORTH

FOREWORD BY SERIES ADVISOR
DR. HENRY LOUIS GATES, JR.

 Enslow Publishers, Inc.
40 Industrial Road   PO Box 38
Box 398   Aldershot
Berkeley Heights, NJ 07922   Hants GU12 6BP
USA   UK

http://www.enslow.com

Library of Congress Cataloging-in-Publication Data

Worth, Richard.
    The slave trade in America : cruel commerce / Richard Worth.
       v. cm. — (Slavery in American history)
    Includes bibliographical references and index.
    Contents: A slave's story—Origins of the slave trade—American slave trade in the 17th
century—American slave trade in the 18th century—The slave trade and the law—Slave trade
within the South—Major centers of internal slave trade—End of the slave trade.
    ISBN 0-7660-2151-3
    1. Slave trade—History—Juvenile literature. 2. Slave trade—United States—History—
Juvenile literature. 3. Slave trade—Africa—History—Juvenile literature. [1. Slave trade—
History. 2. Slave trade—Africa—History.] I. Title.
II. Series.
HT985.W67 2004
382'.44'0973—dc22

                                        2003012079

Illustration Credits: The Art Archive/Eileen Tweedy, pp. 60, 71; Collection of the
Newport Historical Society, p. 47; © Corbis Corporation, p. 29; Enslow Publishers,
Inc., pp. 9, 45, 80; © Hemera Technologies, Inc., pp. 31, 35, 41, 51; © Jane Reed,
Harvard News Office, p. 5; The John Carter Brown Library at Brown University, pp. 26,
39; Library of Congress, Washington, D.C., USA/Bridgeman Art Library, p. 42; Mary
Evans Picture Library, pp. 21, 24, 38, 49, 53, 56, 93; National Archives and Records
Administration, p. 91; Reproduced from the Collections of the Library of Congress,
pp. 1, 3, 6–7, 15, 67, 75, 83, 98, 101, 111; T/Maker Company/Brøderbund Software,
Inc., p. 55; Wilberforce House, Hull City Museums and Art Galleries, UK/Bridgeman
Art, p. 36.

Cover Illustration: By Permission of the British Library (Background Map);
Reproduced from the Collections of the Library of Congress (B&W Image).

❖ C O N T E N T S ❖

FOREWORD BY SERIES ADVISOR
HENRY LOUIS GATES, JR.   4

1 STORIES OF THE
SLAVE TRADE   7

2 ORIGINS OF THE
SLAVE TRADE 11

3 THE SLAVE TRADE
IN THE 1600s. 27

4 THE SLAVE TRADE
IN THE 1700s. 44

5 THE SLAVE TRADE
AND THE LAW 58

6 SLAVE TRADE WITHIN
THE SOUTH 73

7 MAJOR CENTERS OF INTERNAL
SLAVE TRADE 89

8 END OF THE SLAVE TRADE 104

TIMELINE 114

CHAPTER NOTES 116

GLOSSARY 123

FURTHER READING 124

INTERNET ADDRESSES
AND HISTORIC SITES 125

INDEX 126

American Slavery's Undying Legacy

While the Thirteenth Amendment outlawed slavery in the United States in 1865, the impact of that institution continued to be felt long afterward, and in many ways is still being felt today. The broad variety of experiences encompassed within that epoch of American history can be difficult to encapsulate. Enslaved, free, owner, trader, abolitionist: each "category" hides a complexity of experience as varied as the number of individuals who occupied these identities.

One thing is certain: in spite of how slavery has sometimes been portrayed, very few, if any, enslaved blacks were utter victims who quietly and passively accepted such circumstances. Those who claimed ownership over Africans and African Americans used violence, intimidation, and other means to wield a great degree of power and control. But as human beings—and as laborers within an economic system that depended on labor—all enslaved blacks retained varying degrees of agency within that system.

The "Slavery in American History" series provides a strong and needed overview of the most important aspects of American slavery, from the first transport of African slaves to the American colonies, to the long fight for abolition, to the lasting impact of slavery on America's economy, politics, and culture. Only by understanding American slavery and its complex legacies can we begin to understand the challenge facing not just African Americans, but all Americans: To make certain that our country is a living and breathing embodiment of the principles enunciated in the Constitution of the United States. Only by understanding the past can we mend the present and ensure the rights of our future generations.

—**Henry Louis Gates, Jr.**, *Ph.D., W.E.B. Du Bois Professor of the Humanities, Chair of the Department African and African-American Studies, Director of the W.E.B. Du Bois Institute for African and African-American Research, Harvard University.*

Dr. Henry Louis Gates, Jr., Series Advisor

Dr. Henry Louis Gates, Jr., is author of a number of books including: *The Trials of Phillis Wheatley: America's First Poet and Her Encounters with the Founding Fathers, The African-American Century* (with Cornel West), *Little Known Black History Facts, Africana: The Encyclopedia of the African American Experience, Wonders of the African*

World, The Future of The Race (with Cornel West), *Colored People: A Memoir, Loose Cannons: Notes on the Culture Wars, The Signifying Monkey: Towards A Theory of Afro-American Literary Criticism, Figures in Black: Words, Signs, and the Racial Self,* and *Thirteen Ways of Looking at a Black Man.*

Professor Gates earned his M.A. and Ph.D. in English Literature from Clare College at the University of Cambridge. Before beginning his work at Harvard in 1991, he taught at Yale, Cornell, and Duke universities. He has been named one of *Time* magazine's "25 Most Influential Americans," received a National Humanities Medal, and was elected to the American Academy of Arts and Letters.

CHAPTER 1

STORIES OF THE SLAVE TRADE

Venture Smith was born under a different name about 1729 in Guinea, located in West Africa. His father was a wealthy prince of the Dukandara people. However, his people were attacked by a neighboring tribe. He was captured, tortured, and killed.

At the age of six, Venture Smith was then led off with a "rope put about my neck."[1] He was taken on a journey of about four hundred miles. He was forced to carry a huge stone on his head. Eventually, he reached the coast where he was sold to a slave ship from Rhode Island. "I was bought on board by one Robert Mumford . . . for four gallons of rum . . . and called Venture, on account of his having purchased me with his own private venture [money]. Thus I came by my name."[2] Venture Smith was part of a triangular trade. Rum and other products from New England were traded for slaves. They were then taken to the New World and sold to sugarcane planters. The planters, in turn, traded sugar and molasses to the slavers who brought these products to New England, where they were used to make rum.

During the eighteenth century, thousands of slaves were transported to America. Dr. Alexander Falconbridge observed some of them while he worked as a surgeon onboard slave ships. Slaves were often brought aboard ship in handcuffs and leg irons. The men and women were separated. They were kept below decks in such a small space that the slaves could not stand up. If the weather was calm, the slaves were brought up on deck in the morning. They were usually fed twice a day. The slave traders realized that every healthy slave would bring a large sum of money. However, some slaves refused to eat. They were very unhappy about being aboard a slave ship and taken away from their homes in Africa. "Upon the Negroes refusing to take sustenance," Falconbridge recalled, "I have seen coals of fire, glowing hot, put on a shovel and placed so near their lips as to scorch and burn them. And this has been accompanied with threats of forcing them to swallow the coals if they any longer persisted in refusing to eat."[3]

The slavers also tried to force the Africans to get exercise by dancing on deck. Any slaves who refused

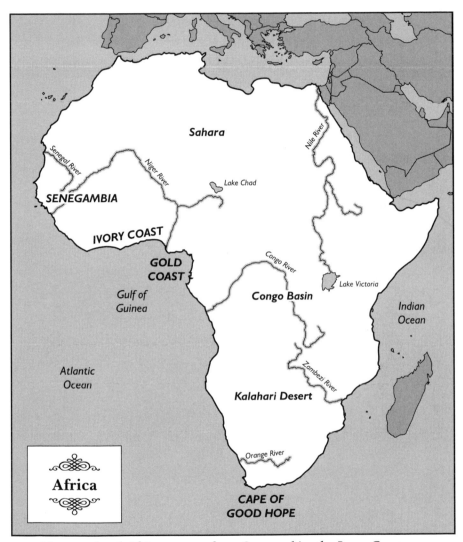

Africa

Many enslaved Africans came from Senegambia, the Ivory Coast, or the Gold Coast. Some also came from the interior of Africa.

were whipped. The slaves were then taken back below deck, where the conditions were often intolerable. As Falconbridge reported, there was very little fresh air, and the slaves regularly developed illnesses, such as "fevers . . . which generally carries off great numbers of them."[4]

Those slaves who arrived in the New World were sold to planters. They were forced to work on plantations growing sugarcane, cotton and rice.

Over five centuries, millions of slaves were transported from Africa to the New World. Slaves were kidnapped and loaded on ships for terrible sea voyages. Frequently separated from family, many slaves died under the brutal conditions of the plantations, while others resisted the system. The slave trade was a harsh endeavor that enslaved generations of Africans and African Americans.

ORIGINS OF THE SLAVE TRADE

THE SLAVE TRADE BEGAN IN THE ANCIENT world. During the first and second centuries B.C., Roman armies rounded up and enslaved people whom they conquered, such as the Germans or the Gauls. These included women, children, and warriors who had fought against the Romans in battle. Some of these slaves became servants in the households of wealthy Roman aristocrats. Others went to work on huge farms in Italy and other parts of the Roman empire. These farms grew crops, such as wheat and barley, that were necessary to feed the people of Italy. By the end of the first century A.D., the area of present-day Italy included 2 to 3 million slaves, which comprised approximately 35 to 40 percent of the entire Italian population.[1]

Medieval Slave Trade

Eventually, European tribes, such as the Huns and the Visigoths, became more powerful than the Roman armies. As these tribes invaded the Roman empire in the fourth and fifth centuries A.D., the large Roman farms were abandoned. The numbers of slaves who were working the farms declined. However, the slave trade continued in Europe during the Middle Ages (c. A.D. 500–1500). Battles regularly occurred among different tribes. As one tribe defeated another, it enslaved the conquered people. During the eighth century, for example, the Frankish (German) ruler Charlemagne created a large empire in western Europe. Throughout the empire, conquered peoples were enslaved. Slaves were sold at great fairs in towns, such as Verdun in France.[2]

Meanwhile, a powerful new empire was being built in the Middle East and North Africa by the Muslims. These were followers of the prophet Muhammad. He was born in Mecca, located in the modern-day country of Saudi Arabia. About A.D. 570, Muhammad founded one of the world's major religions called Islam. After Muhammad's death in 632, the Muslims began to expand their power in the Middle East. They conquered North Africa, enslaving many of the people who lived there. Then, during the eighth century, the Muslims invaded Spain. Here, they conquered the kingdom of the Visigoths and enslaved them. The new slaves served in Muslim palaces and worked on farms.

In North Africa, Muslim merchants developed a profitable trade in black slaves. They were purchased from tribes in western and central Africa and transported across the Sahara Desert to ports along the coast. In addition to slaves, the merchants also bought and sold gold and ivory from Africa. A brisk slave trade was also conducted by Italian merchants from cities such as Genoa and Venice. Slaves from Russia and Hungary were sold by these merchants to Italian aristocrats and other wealthy nobles who lived in towns along the Mediterranean coast.

On Mediterranean islands, such as Cyprus, Sicily, and Crete, Italian merchants also established large sugar plantations, which flourished during the latter part of the Middle Ages. These plantations were cultivated by slaves as well as free peasants. As historian Herbert Klein has written: "The techniques of sugar production and slave plantation agriculture that developed . . . in the New World had their origins in the eastern Mediterranean in the . . . Middle Ages."[3]

Rise of Portuguese Slave Traders
Throughout the Middle Ages, Christian leaders on the Spanish peninsula slowly conquered the Muslim strongholds. By the beginning of the fifteenth century,

the Muslims controlled only the kingdom of Granada in southern Spain. Meanwhile, the Portuguese people, under King John I, invaded North Africa and captured the important Muslim city of Ceuta. It was located on the north coast of Africa along the Mediterranean. This became part of a new empire being built by the Portuguese. Led by John's brother, Prince Henry, Portuguese ships also began to explore the west coast of Africa.

Prince Henry established his headquarters at Sagres, in southwestern Portugal, early in the fifteenth century. From this position, his sea captains sailed west and took control of the islands of Madeira and the Azores. Gradually, they sailed southward along the coast of Africa. The Portuguese explorers were primarily interested in finding gold, which had been bought in the past by Muslim traders. Huge deposits were reportedly located in the African interior. By sailing along the coast and finding a route inland along West Africa's rivers, the Portuguese hoped to bypass the Muslim traders. Thus, Portugal could gain control of the rich African trade and create a wealthy empire.

As the Portuguese people searched for gold, they also began to take control of the slave trade. The Portuguese explorers seized Africans from the villages along the coast. They were brought to Portugal, where they served in aristocratic households and worked the

Slaves were transported through the interior of Africa by Portuguese slave hunters.

sugar plantations. These plantations had been established in the southern part of the country. The first African slaves arrived in Portugal in 1444. There were 235 of them. One observer who saw them working in the fields wrote:

> What heart could be so hard as not to be pierced with piteous feeling to see that company? For some kept their heads low, and their faces bathed in tears, looking one upon another. Others stood groaning very dolorously, looking up to the height of heaven, fixing their

eyes upon it, crying out loudly, as if asking help from the Father of nature; others struck their faces with the palms of their hands, throwing themselves at full length upon the ground. . . .[4]

The misery of these slaves, however, was not enough to stop the Portuguese from expanding the slave trade. In the past, Muslim merchants had supplied slaves to large auctions in Portugal. Now the Portuguese people could provide their own slaves. In addition, the government profited from the trade. Portuguese monarchs were entitled to one-fifth of everything that was brought into the country from abroad.

As the Portuguese sailed southward during the fifteenth century, they encountered the major rivers of western Africa. These included the Senegal, the Gambia, the Niger, and the Congo. The Portuguese ships were often small. Many were caravels, ships with only one deck and a square sail. They carried about one hundred slaves.

The Portuguese had hoped to sail along the African rivers into the heartland of the continent. However, they were prevented from undertaking these explorations by the conditions in the interior. Diseases, such as malaria and yellow fever, struck down the Portuguese who ventured along the rivers. These tropical diseases, carried by mosquitoes, are often fatal.

The Portuguese explorers were forced to anchor at the mouths of the rivers. At first, they seized African villagers along the coast and transported them back to Portugal as slaves. The Portuguese had superior weapons, including guns and metal swords. After learning of the intentions of the Portuguese, the Africans used their wooden boats to escape from the kidnappers. They also traded for European weapons and beat back the Portuguese. In order to obtain more slaves, the Portuguese realized that they would need to trade for them instead of simply kidnapping them.

Gradually, a brisk trade sprung up between the Portuguese explorers and the Africans along the coast. Much of this trade was controlled by local African rulers. African rulers regularly engaged in wars with each other and captured slaves from rival tribes. With the arrival of the Portuguese, the slaves were also sold to them for European manufactured goods. These included bracelets, swords, candles, and woolen shawls.[5] Africans also liked colorful printed cloth. The Portuguese were opening up new trading markets in India. From these markets, they bought Indian printed cotton, transported it to Africa, and exchanged it for slaves. Some of these slaves were taken to the island of Madeira, where the Portuguese had established sugar plantations. By the end of the fifteenth century, Portugal exported more sugar than any other area of

Europe.[6] In addition, the Portuguese also developed sugar plantations on the islands of São Tomé and Principe in the Gulf of Guinea in western Africa. An estimated eight hundred to two thousand slaves per year were taken off the African continent by the end of the fifteenth century.[7]

Meanwhile, the Portuguese began building a string of trading posts along the coast of West Africa during the early sixteenth century. These trading posts were designed to help them protect their slave trade. They also befriended local African rulers. The Portuguese developed a close relationship with the king of the Kongo, Affonso I. He controlled the local slave trade. King Affonso allowed the Portuguese to build a fort at Luanda, located in modern Angola, during the latter part of the sixteenth century. While some slaves were transported to the Portuguese plantations, others were traded to African rulers elsewhere along the coast. Slavery had long been practiced by African tribes. In fact, slaves were considered a form of wealth among well-to-do Africans. In return for these slaves, the Portuguese explorers often received gold. In an area called the Gold Coast, in the present-day country of Ghana, Portuguese traders purchased gold from Africans. This gold came from mines located further inland. Late in the fifteenth century, the Portuguese

SOURCE DOCUMENT

Sir, there is in our kingdom, a great obstacle to God. Many of our subjects crave the Portuguese merchandise which your people bring to our kingdom so keenly. In order to satisfy their crazy appetite they snatch our free subjects, or people who have been freed.

They even take noblemen and the sons of noblemen, even our kinsmen. They sell them to white men who are in our kingdom, after having transported their prisoners on the sly in the dead of night. Then the prisoners are branded. The white men . . . cannot say from whom they have bought the prisoners.[8]

In a letter to King Henry of Portugal, King Affonso expresses his concern that the slave trade is growing out of control.

established a fort at Elmina on the Gold Coast, to protect the gold that they had purchased.

The Opening of the New World

While the Portuguese were exploring the coast of Africa, Spain was also beginning its overseas empire. During the early 1490s, Christopher Columbus convinced the Spanish monarchs, King Ferdinand and Queen Isabella, to let him lead a small fleet of ships westward to find a new route to China. Spices and silk had been imported from China throughout the Middle Ages across central Asia. These trade routes were controlled by Italian merchants. The Spanish hoped to bypass the Italians and find a new route to the Far East.

Instead of this route, however, Columbus landed on the island of Hispaniola in the New World in 1492. Thinking he had reached India, Columbus called the people he found there Indians. Columbus noticed that the Indians wore gold jewelry. He hoped that there might be large deposits of gold on the island. Eventually, as the Spaniards colonized other islands in the Caribbean, some gold was discovered. The Spanish began rounding up the Indians and enslaving them to work in the gold mines. In addition, Spanish settlers were given large plots of land called *encomiendas*, along with a number of enslaved Indians who were forced to farm the land.

The Caribbean Indians were treated harshly. Many died while working in the mines or on the Spanish estates. In addition, the Indians were infected by new diseases that had never existed in the New World. These included measles and smallpox, which were brought to the Caribbean islands by the Spanish. Because the Indians' immune systems had no tolerance

Spaniards on the island of Hispaniola worked most of the Caribbean Indians there to death. Needing another source of labor, they began importing slaves from Guinea, Africa, to work in their gold mines.

of these diseases, thousands died. As a result, the Spanish found themselves without enough slave laborers to work their mines and their estates.

During the first quarter of the sixteenth century, African slaves began to be shipped to the New World. Sugar plantations were being established on Hispaniola, Cuba, and Puerto Rico. Africans were brought in to work on these plantations, just as they did in Portugal or on São Tomé off the coast of Africa. They also worked in the Cuban gold mines.

Meanwhile, the Spanish had been expanding their empire in the New World. During the 1520s, the conquistador Hernán Cortés had conquered the Aztec empire in Mexico. In the following decade, Francisco Pizarro defeated the Incas, who controlled a vast empire that stretched across the modern countries of Peru, Chile, and Ecuador. More gold and silver mines were discovered.

At the Potosi mine in Peru, there were huge deposits of silver. Africans were transported from the area between the Senegal and Gambia rivers to work the mines. Many slaves were also exported from the Portuguese trading center at Luanda. Slaves were used to pan for gold that was found in the rivers of Peru and in other areas of South America. Meanwhile, the Portuguese had been settling a colony in Brazil during the first half of the sixteenth century. Here, the colonists began to develop huge sugar plantations to supply the European markets. These plantations called for a steady supply of slaves.

Historian Hugh Thomas estimates that approximately forty thousand slaves were sent to the New World in the second quarter of the sixteenth century. This number rose to sixty thousand over the following twenty-five years.[9] At first, these slaves were primarily transported by the Portuguese. Then, the Spanish king allowed other nations to carry slaves to the Spanish empire. In 1580, the Spanish king Philip II took control of Portugal. The Portuguese lost the slave trade. But other nations, such as England, France, and the Netherlands, still supplied some of the slaves to the Spanish empire.

A Slave Empire

The Spanish empire in the New World depended on slavery. As historian Herbert Klein has pointed out, there were too few people in Europe to be sent to America to work the plantations there. During the late Middle Ages, Europe had been struck by the Black Death. This was a plague carried to humans by fleas that lived on rats. The plague wiped out as many as one third of the European population.[10] As a result, there was a shortage of labor in Europe. As the economy began to expand during the following centuries, western Europe needed all the people available to work in growing industries.[11]

The solution for the new empire developing in America was to import African slaves. They seemed to be an excellent source of labor for the sugar plantations, just as they had been in the past on Cyprus or Crete. Slaves dug the holes with hoes to plant the sugarcane, then approximately fifteen months later

Slaves in the Caribbean had to weather the extreme heat while harvesting sugarcane.

harvested the crop. They cut the large cane stalks with machetes. Then, the cane was taken to mills, where it was ground to produce juice and turned into sugar or molasses. The molasses was often used to produce rum. "The ideal sugar plantation seemed to be about 750 acres, certainly not less than 300 acres," wrote historian Hugh Thomas. "The enterprise was best carried out with, say, 120 slaves, 40 oxen, and a great house in the center, surrounded by . . . slaves' quarters. On such properties, slavery, black African slavery, appeared the best kind of labor."[12]

The slave traders followed various routes from the African coast to the New World. Slaves purchased from Africans might first be taken to São Tomé or to the huge fortress that had been built at Elmina. In this large castle, hundreds of slaves were held before being sent to the New World. In other fortresses, slaves were kept in underground prisons. There was little fresh air for them to breathe, and many died of disease. Those who survived would be shipped to the Cape Verde Islands and finally to the Caribbean and South America. There, they would be sold to planters to work on the plantations. The slaves would grow sugarcane, tobacco, or other crops. Some slaves worked in the mines. Others were used to construct buildings, build roads, and erect bridges.

During the last part of the sixteenth century, the

Slave-trading companies constructed large castles on the African coast. Slaves were held in these castles until they could be rowed out to towering slave ships that waited in the churning sea.

Spanish king Philip II arranged for 188 ships to carry slaves to the New World. About half of these ships brought slaves from Guinea in central Africa, totaling 5,500 slaves per year.[13] These slaves did the hard work in the mines and on the plantations in the Spanish empire. Shortly afterward, slaves would also begin to appear elsewhere in the New World—in the newly established English colonies of the Caribbean and North America.

THE SLAVE TRADE
IN THE 1600s

S PAIN AND PORTUGAL WERE NOT THE ONLY
countries that could make profits in the
slave trade. In fact, during the 1600s, Britain, France,
and the Netherlands would become the dominant
slave traders between Africa and parts of America,
including the North American colonies.

The Dutch Traders
During the early part of the seventeenth century,
Dutch traders began to send their ships to the West
African coast to collect slaves and transport them to
America. In 1619, a Dutch ship brought a shipment of
Africans to North America. Carrying twenty Africans,
the ship put in at Jamestown, Virginia, and sold the
cargo to the farmers there. North America, however,
was a very small market for the Dutch. They were far

more interested in bringing slaves to the islands of the Caribbean and the rich colony of Brazil.

In 1621, Dutch merchants established the West India Company. At first, their ships raided Portuguese slave traders, took the Africans, and sold them in the Americas. Gradually, the Dutch also established their own forts on the west coast of Africa and captured Portuguese forts. In North America, the Dutch established a colony at New Amsterdam (later called New York, when it was captured by the English in 1664). Slaves first arrived in New Amsterdam in 1625.

By the 1650s, Dutch merchants in New Amsterdam were sailing for West Africa. They were carrying on a brisk slave trade. In 1654, for example, traders named Jan de Sweerts and Dirck Pieterson sailed their ship to Africa and returned with a load of slaves. Another ship, the *St. John*, picked up 219 slaves from the African coast in 1659. The *King Solomon*, which also made the journey in 1659, brought 331 slaves to the Caribbean island of Curaçao. And in 1664, the Dutch ship *Gideon* brought over 300 slaves to New Amsterdam.[1]

English Slave Traders

Like the Dutch, English merchants also participated in the slave trade during the seventeenth century. At first, they attacked Spanish and Portuguese raiders in the Caribbean. To do this successfully, however, the

Dutch traders brought the first Africans to Jamestown, Virginia, on a warship called a man-of-war.

English needed to establish bases for their operations. In 1624, a group of English adventurers landed on St. Kitts, an island in the Caribbean. With the help of French allies, they defeated the Caribbean Indians and divided the island between them. Around the same time, the English also established a colony on Barbados. Gradually, settlers were drawn to both islands. At first, they grew tobacco. There was an enormous demand for it in Europe. The planters on Barbados also began growing cotton. Finally, they turned to growing sugar on large plantations.

The English tried to recruit indentured servants to work these plantations. These indentured workers agreed to serve the planters for a specified period of time, often five to ten years. They worked to pay off debts and for their passage to the New World. In order to acquire all the indentured servants they needed, the planters agreed to take criminals from the English prisons. In addition, some workers were kidnapped from their towns in England. They were taken to waiting ships and transported to the colony.

But, as the demand for sugar grew, the indentured servants were not plentiful enough to supply all the labor demands on Barbados. In addition, conditions had changed in England. This slowed the flow of indentured servants. First, wages had increased at home, making employment there more attractive.

Second, a period of
civil war had come to
an end, so people
were more interested
in remaining in England. The bloody civil war had torn
England apart during the 1640s. It began when the
English Parliament, led by a religious group called
the Puritans, rebelled against the illegal policies of King
Charles I. In 1649, after King Charles was executed by
the Puritans, the government was directed by their
leader, Oliver Cromwell. However, turmoil in England
continued. After Cromwell's death, Charles II became
king, and a period of peace returned to England.

As a result of improving conditions in England and
an inadequate supply of indentured servants, the
planters of Barbados began importing African slaves.
At first, they were supplied by the Dutch. However, in
1672, the Royal African Company was founded. It was
given a monopoly, or complete control, of the slave
trade to the English colonics by the government of
King Charles II. The company established outposts in
Africa. These outposts were built along the area known
as the Gold Coast. From here, the Royal African
Company began to trade for slaves. In addition, slaves
were acquired in the coastal section between the Volta
and Niger rivers, which was known as the Slave Coast.
Over the next two decades, the Royal African Company

would export approximately ninety thousand slaves to America. More than 25 percent of them went to Barbados. Another 25 percent went to the British colony of Jamaica, which was also becoming a large sugar-growing area.[2]

Meanwhile, English merchants were also transporting slaves to North America. But these slaves were only arriving in small numbers. Massachusetts, for example, had only about one hundred slaves in 1680. In Virginia, Maryland, and Carolina (present-day North and South Carolina), approximately ten thousand slaves were brought in between 1670 and 1700.[3] The English colonies were still relying, to a large degree, on indentured servants to work the large tobacco plantations and other estates. But, as in the Caribbean, the supply of servants was drying up.

In Carolina, more and more slaves were beginning to appear. This colony was settled by planters from Barbados. Indeed, Sir John Yeamans, the first governor, was a Barbados planter. He and those like him were accustomed to having slaves work their lands. Yeamans arrived with some of his own slaves. And the planters who came after him also brought slaves to work their lands. At first the settlers planted indigo. Gradually this was replaced by rice growing in the Carolinas. Planters demanded more and more slaves. The Carolinas traded directly with the British colonies

SOURCE DOCUMENT

From *The Fundamental Constitutions of Carolina* (1669):

Every freeman of Carolina shall have absolute power and authority over his negro slaves, of what opinion or religion soever.[4]

From *The First Treatise of Government* (1690):

Slavery is so vile and miserable an Estate of Man, and so directly opposite to the generous Temper and Courage of our Nation; that 'tis hardly to be conceived, that an Englishman, much less a Gentleman, should plead for't.[5]

Philosopher John Locke was an investor in the Royal African Company and wrote *The Fundamental Constitutions of Carolina,* which allowed for slavery. However, Locke also spoke out against slavery in *The First Treatise of Government.*

in the Caribbean, such as Barbados and St. Kitts. They sent timber to the islanders in return for sugar and slaves.

The Growth of the Slave Trade

In the eyes of many planters, slaves seemed to offer a better alternative than indentured servants. The planters who came from Barbados knew that thousands of slaves could be used successfully by local planters to work their plantations. While indentured servants had to be released after a few years and replaced by others, slaves could often be held in bondage for a lifetime. In addition, their offspring were also considered the property of the white masters. As more slaves were being supplied by the British traders, the price of slaves also began to decline. This made them a better investment.

The English traders became very successful at reaping large profits from the slave trade. According to one estimate, the traders realized a 10 percent profit from the slaves they bought and sold. This was considered a good profit for the period.[6] Some experts believe that the profits were even higher, approximately 30 percent.[7] The costs involved were considerable. A merchant had to outfit a ship, hire a crew, and find a captain. The captain usually received a percentage of the profits, about 2 to 5 percent.[8] Then, the merchant had to buy trading goods for the African traders from whom the slaves would be purchased. A merchant also had to pay taxes to the local African ruler to trade for slaves in his area.

Frequently a ship had to spend many months along the African coast picking up a full cargo of slaves. Storms might strike that could damage a ship or even sink it, destroying a slave trader's entire investment and killing hundreds of Africans. The slaves bought by the Royal African Company, for example, often came from the interior of Africa. Small boats would be put over the side of a  large sailing ship. These boats would be rowed up the rivers by the crew to nearby towns where they would trade with Africans for slaves. The European merchants might buy men and women who had been captured as a result of warfare. Indeed, some tribes went to war or made raids on neighboring towns simply to obtain slaves who could be sold to the European traders. Sometimes, a person who had committed a crime, such as theft, was punished by being sold as a slave. People might also be kidnapped and sold into slavery.

A slave who was taken off from his village might be bought and sold several times by various African traders before reaching the coast. There, the slaves were examined to ensure that they were healthy. Then, they were often branded with hot irons. Sometimes,

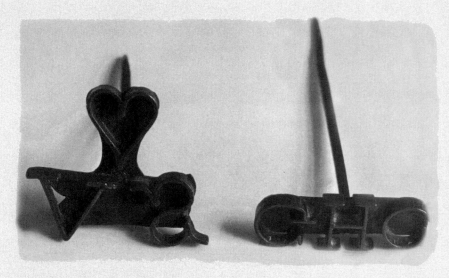

Slaves were often burned with painfully hot branding irons. Each different type of branding iron represented a slave trader or slave-trading company.

the slaves were loaded directly onto a waiting ship. But they might also be kept in small posts, called factories. These were run by employees, or factors, of the Royal African Company.

The company maintained a large factory on the Gold Coast called Cabo Corso. It was protected by stout walls and manned with soldiers. Large quarters, called a barracoon, had been built to house as many as fifteen slaves. However, many factories were much smaller. One employee of the company described a factory this way:

Our factory . . . lies about three miles from the seaside. . . . It stands low near the marshes, which renders it a very unhealthy place to live in. The white men the African Company send there seldom [return] to tell their tale. 'Tis compass'd round with a mud wall about six feet high, and on the southside is the gate; within is a large yard, a mud thatch'd house, where the factor lives, with the white men; also a storehouse, a [place] for slaves, and a place where they bury the dead white men. . . .

Because of the marshes, the mosquitoes at the factory were almost unbearable: "I had not lain down above an hour in the factor's bed, but I was so vex'd and tormented by those little malicious animals that I was forced to get up again and dress myself, put gloves on my hands, and tie a handkerchief over my face till day-light. . . ."[9]

The life of a slave in a barracoon at one of these factories was often miserable. As historian Daniel Mannix wrote:

The barracoon was a stockade [jail] within the [factory] and resembled a corral for cattle. A long shed ran down the center to protect the slaves from sun and rain. Down the middle of the shed was stretched a long chain fastened to a stake at either end, the men slaves being secured at intervals along the chain. The women and children were allowed to run loose. At one corner of the barracoon was usually a tower where an armed guard kept watch over the slaves.[10]

Slaves might also be housed aboard a slave ship.

Until they could be put on a ship, slaves were held in Africa in a barracoon. There they were chained together and often whipped.

Hundreds of slaves might be forced to live in a ship for months while it cruised the African coast looking for more captives. Once a ship was full of slaves, it was ready to begin the voyage across the Atlantic. This was called the Middle Passage. As historian Peter Kolchin explained:

> Men were usually kept in chains; women and children, fewer in number, were sometimes allowed greater freedom of movement. In ships run by "tight packers," who deplored the waste of space provided by holds five feet high and who consequently installed middle shelves, creating two levels of two and a half feet, slaves were often crammed together so closely they could barely move.[11]

After Africans were sold to a slave trader, they were rowed to the slave
ship in a small boat.

Slave-ship captains tried to ensure that there was enough food and water on board to keep the slaves alive. After all, it was in their best interest to deliver as many slaves as possible to the plantations. Still, many died on the journey. Death estimates range from a low of 5 percent to over 30 percent.[12] Slaves might not have received enough water to be kept alive in the hot, crowded conditions below decks. Death also occurred from diseases. These included malaria, measles, yellow fever, and dysentery. Known as the "bloody flux," dysentery causes diarrhea, fever, and often death.

For the Africans, the trip across the Atlantic was a miserable experience. It began as they left the shores of their homeland. As Thomas Phillips, who sailed on the slave ship *Hannibal* during the late seventeenth century from London, wrote:

> The Negroes are so . . . loth [unhappy] to leave their own country, that they have often leap'd out of the . . . ship, into the sea, and kept under water till they were drowned, to avoid being taken up and saved by our boats, which pursued them; they having a more dreadful apprehension of [America] than we can have of hell. . . .[13]

On this particular voyage, the ship lost 320 slaves because of a serious epidemic that broke out on the ship.[14]

The same illnesses that afflicted the slaves also affected the crews on the slave ships. Many ships had crews of about thirty to forty sailors.[15] The *Hannibal,* for example, lost fourteen of its crew, a very high number. There were also reports of captains treating their crews harshly. As one

man who served aboard a slaver recalled:

> A young man on board one of the ships was frequently beaten in a very severe manner, for very trifling faults. This was done sometimes with what is termed a cat [a rope with nine branches and knots on each branch] and sometimes he was beaten with a bamboo. Being one day cruelly beaten with the latter, the poor lad, unable to endure the severe usage, leaped out of one of the gun ports . . . into the river. [He was caught,] and his head forced into a tub of water, which had been left there for the negro women to wash their hands in. In this situation he was kept until he was nearly suffocated. . . .[16]

Trade Back and Forth Across the Atlantic

After the slaves reached America, merchants displayed them in their storehouses. Buyers would come in and examine the slaves to ensure that they were fit. A buyer might feel a slave's limbs and look in his mouth to see if his teeth were healthy. If the buyer were satisfied, he might make an offer for the slave. Sometimes, slaves would also be sold at an auction. Unfortunately,

Africans suffered inside the hold of a slave ship. This illustration depicts the hold of the *Gloria*.

conditions in the warehouses were often as bad as aboard the ships. Slaves were crowded together, often without enough food and water. As a result, some died.

Meanwhile, the slave ships were preparing for a return trip across the Atlantic. Once the *Hannibal* had unloaded its slaves, it was loaded with cotton, ginger, and sugar, and returned to England.[17] Most merchants liked to pick up a cargo for their return voyage so they could make money on both ends of the trip. The slavers also participated in a huge triangular trade that began to spring up across the Atlantic. Merchants would load up trade goods in Europe. These goods would then be taken to Africa, where they would be bartered for slaves. The slaves would then be transported to America and exchanged for other goods. These included tobacco, rice, sugar, and rum, which were brought back to Europe. However, it would be incorrect to imagine that every voyage was part of the triangular trade. Some merchants traded back and forth between Africa and America. Others could not find a cargo on their return trip from America to Europe. In addition, ships involved in carrying goods were often different from slavers—they were larger and used only for transporting goods, not slaves.[18]

Slave Trade at the End of the Century

By the end of the seventeenth century, the slave trade to North America was growing, but it still made up just a tiny portion of the entire Atlantic slave trade. However, as tobacco plantations increased in Virginia and Maryland, the number of slaves increased, too. In 1680, for example, there were an estimated four thousand African slaves on these plantations. By the beginning of the next century, that number was five times larger. Indeed, slaves had become about 40 percent of the people living in Virginia and about 23 percent of Maryland's population.[19] During the 1700s, the population of slaves would grow much larger and American ships would play a much larger role in the slave trade.

CHAPTER 4

THE SLAVE TRADE
IN THE 1700s

AARON LOPEZ WAS BORN IN PORTUGAL. During the eighteenth century, he came to Newport, Rhode Island, where he opened a shop that sold a variety of items. Eventually, he took the money he made and invested in the slave trade. He had thirty ships, which traveled regularly to Africa and the West Indies. Lopez became one of the wealthiest merchants in Newport. He built a magnificent mansion and entertained his friends at lavish parties. However, in the process, he robbed many Africans of their freedom, making them suffer the dreaded Middle Passage.

The merchants of Newport were involved in a vast triangular trade. Distilleries in Rhode Island and other parts of New England made a brand of rum that was highly valued in Africa. They transported rum to the African coast. There, they traded the rum for slaves,

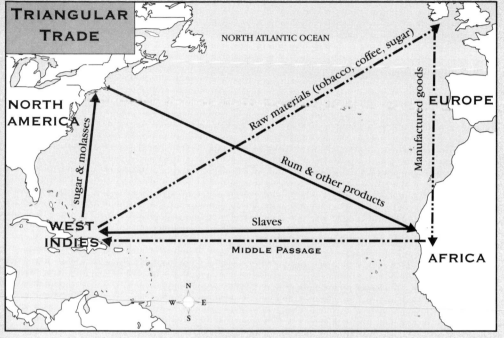

The sale of slaves to the New World was just part of the vast triangular trade that involved many different countries.

paying two hundred gallons per slave.[1] Sometimes, the traders would try to get a better price by watering down the rum and cheating the Africans.

The slaves were then transported to the West Indies and sold to sugar planters. In the Indies, the Newport merchants picked up cargoes of sugar and molasses. Then, they transported the sugar and molasses to New England, where they were manufactured into rum.

Newport's merchants had begun this profitable trade in about 1725. There was very little land in Rhode Island, a tiny colony. Instead of becoming farmers, the inhabitants had to look for other types of work. According to one estimate, over nine hundred ships were involved in the slave trade at one time or another. And they brought over one hundred thousand slaves to the New World.[2] The Newport ships were called "rum-men" because they only carried rum, instead of other kinds of trade goods carried by British and French slavers. The ships from Newport were smaller than the vessels that sailed from England. As a result, slave captains had to pack the slaves more tightly. Some slaves died as a result. As one captain wrote: ". . . my slaves was all taken with the flucks [flux], so that I could not sell them; lost three with it and have three more very bad. . . ."[3]

The Middle Passage took anywhere from five weeks to three months, depending on the weather. Slaves often died due to illness. The ships had small crews to save money. So, the slaves were constantly chained throughout the voyage to prevent them from starting a mutiny. Sometimes mutinies did occur, especially when a large number of the crew had died from disease. But the slavers were willing to take the risk. The profits could be large. While many slaves were

Newport, Rhode Island, was one of the American colonies' biggest slave-trading ports.

transported to the plantations in the West Indies, others were brought to North America.

Slave Trading Centers

In addition to Newport, there were other slave trading centers in New England. These included Boston, Massachusetts; New London, Connecticut; and Bristol, Rhode Island. Another important slave port was New York City, which sent out over one hundred trading missions to Africa during the middle of the eighteenth century.[4] Besides the triangular trade, merchants in

New York and elsewhere traded directly with the West Indies. They bought slaves and transported them to North America. Between 1700 and 1730, for example, 70 percent of the slaves being transported to New York came from the Caribbean. Many of these slaves went to work on the large estates located outside the city.

Another major port for the slave trade was Charleston, South Carolina. Among the premier traders in this city was Henry Laurens. A partner in the firm of Austen and Laurens, Henry traded in a variety of goods. These included wine, rice, and indigo. But slaves were probably the most profitable.

As the slave ships approached the coast of South Carolina, they stopped at Sullivan's Island, outside the city of Charleston. There the slaves were checked for disease, before being allowed to set foot on the mainland. Once they arrived at Lauren's slave mart, they were auctioned off to planters from South Carolina, Georgia, and even the Spanish territory of East Florida. Indeed, an estimated 40 percent of the slaves that arrived in North America during the eighteenth century came through the port of Charleston.[5] Laurens traded directly with Africa for some of his slaves. However, he purchased many of them from English merchants who had bought the slaves and loaded them onto their own ships.

Because the North American colonies were part of

the British empire, by far the largest number of slaves were carried by English ships. During the 1720s, English merchants carried an estimated ten thousand slaves to English colonies on the eastern seaboard of North America. This number increased to forty thousand in the next decade, and seventy thousand by the 1760s.[6] Because the number of slaves along the African coast had declined after years of trading, slave traders began to search farther inland. Slaves were often kidnapped, chained together, and brought to the coast.

Men, women, and children were often captured in central Africa, then transported over land to the coast.

Where the Slaves Went

Some slaves were shipped to the northern colonies. Here they worked as household servants, craftspeople and artisans, and farm workers. But the number of Africans in the North was only about 15 percent of the total population of settlers there.[7] Most of the slaves worked in the southern colonies, such as Maryland, Virginia, the Carolinas, and later Georgia. Indeed, there were more Africans among the population of South Carolina than white settlers.

In South Carolina, the slaves worked on the rice and indigo plantations. Rice cultivation had begun about the beginning of the eighteenth century. The warm climate and swamplands of South Carolina proved to be an ideal climate for growing rice. Many of the slaves who were imported from Africa were already familiar with growing rice, which was also cultivated there. Therefore, they could assist the Carolina planters in irrigating the fields. Because rice growing required extensive irrigation, it was most economical to develop big plantations. These were worked by a large number of slaves. It was backbreaking work. The slaves were also exposed to fatal diseases, such as malaria. By the middle of the eighteenth century, many plantations had over fifty slaves. Some had more than one hundred slaves.[8]

Another lucrative crop was indigo. After the indigo

leaves were harvested, they were put into huge tubs of water and beaten by the slaves. As historian Ira Berlin explains: "The rotting indigo emitted a putrid odor and attracted clouds of

flies that only slaves could be forced to tolerate. In time, the putrefied leaves were removed and the bluish liquid drained into a series of vats, where slaves 'beat' the liquid with broad paddles."[9] Eventually, the liquid turned into mud. This was dried into blocks of indigo and sold to English merchants.

Rice and indigo were not only grown in South Carolina, but also farther south in Georgia. This colony had been founded in 1733 and at first banned the slave trade because the British parliament did not want to expand slavery in North America. But as plantations grew, the ban was eventually abolished in 1750. Slaves were imported to Savannah and auctioned off to Georgia planters.

Slaves were also imported to the Spanish colony of Florida and the French colony of Louisiana. Tobacco, rice, and indigo were grown in Florida. New Orleans, Louisiana, became a center for the slave trade. One French slave ship, the *Venus*, brought over three hundred fifty slaves to New Orleans in 1729. But many of them died of disease.

The Impact of the American Revolution

In 1775, the American Revolution began in North America. The thirteen colonies resented efforts by the British parliament to levy taxes on them. Eventually, delegates from all the colonies supported the Declaration of Independence in 1776. At the beginning of the war, all the colonies permitted slavery. But this situation gradually began to change. The Declaration of Independence declared that "all men are created equal." Some states took this to heart. States such as New Hampshire and Massachusetts started freeing their slaves. Indeed, slavery had never been widespread in these areas during the colonial period. There was no need for slaves on the small farms of northern New England.

In other states, however, where slavery was more critical to the economy, people made no effort to free their slaves. Nevertheless, the war wreaked havoc with the American slave system. The British dominance of the sea cut down the slave trade. As British armies occupied cities such as New York, Charleston, and Savannah, slaves often fled from their masters.

The British colonial governor, Lord Dunmore, promised the African Americans freedom if they fought

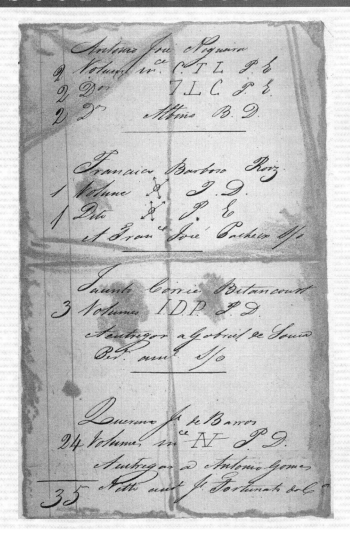

Each slave ship often had a bill of lading that listed the ship's contents. The slaves listed on this bill came from Loanda, Cameroon, in West Africa.

against the rebel armies. This was primarily an attempt to undermine the American economy and persuade their rebellious colonists to ask for peace. Nevertheless, many slaves left the plantations and sought safety behind the British lines. As the war turned against the British in the early 1780s, they retreated from the South. They left cities such as Savannah and Charleston. However, the British took as many as six thousand slaves with them from Savannah and twelve thousand slaves from Charleston.[10]

Once peace returned during the 1780s, northern states began passing laws to free their slaves. These states included Pennsylvania, Connecticut, and Rhode Island. In the southern states, however, slavery remained after the end of the American Revolution. Indigo plantations had largely disappeared. The United States had lost its primary customer, England, as a result of the war. Rice and tobacco, however, continued to be important plantation crops. Some Virginia slaveholders had also moved west. Here they began growing hemp, sugar, and even cotton.

Slave Trade at the End of the Eighteenth Century
At the Constitutional Convention in 1787, the founding fathers debated slavery and the slave trade in Philadelphia. The founders realized that slavery was being abolished in the North and believed it would

eventually disappear in the South. Many of the delegates also wanted to ban the slave trade. In some southern states, such as Virginia and Maryland, slaves were no longer as necessary as they had been in earlier years. The tobacco plantations had exhausted the soil. Planters wanted to sell some of their slaves to states farther south. They believed that if the Atlantic slave trade was banned, they could get a better price for their slaves. However, states such as South Carolina and Georgia threatened to leave the union if the slave trade was abolished. South Carolina and Georgia wanted to import new slaves from Africa to replace those who had left during the American Revolution. So, the founders agreed on a compromise. The transatlantic trade would continue until 1808. After that, it would be prohibited. By 1789, however, most states had already passed laws prohibiting their merchants from bringing slaves into their ports.

Nevertheless, slave traders continued to operate in the Atlantic. Newport had ceased to be the center of the northern slave trade. The city had been occupied by the British during the American Revolution. Traders had been forced to flee. Instead, Bristol, Rhode Island, became the center of the northern slave trade. Its merchants continued to carry slaves to the West Indies.

Slaves were forced to dance on the ship's deck. Traders made the Africans do this so that they would get some exercise and therefore be attractive to buyers in the New World.

In the South, many plantation owners were at first afraid to import more slaves. A slave revolt had succeeded in the French island of Santo Domingo during the 1790s. Southerners feared a similar revolt might occur in their own states if the population of slaves grew any larger. However, while the planters were hesitant to import slaves, the demand for them was growing.

The reason for the rise in demand for slaves was the development of the cotton gin by a Connecticut inventor named Eli Whitney. Invented in 1793, the cotton gin would revolutionize the entire economy of the South. The gin made it possible for a single slave to clean the seeds from fifty times the amount of cotton that he could clean in the past. More powerful water-powered gins would increase the amount of cotton that could be cleaned by a thousand times.[11] Now, more slaves were needed to pick more cotton.

Cotton, like rice, was most economically grown on plantations worked by slaves. Suddenly, cotton became a new crop for making money in the lower South. It was not only grown in the Carolinas and Georgia. Cotton plantations spread westward as Americans moved into Alabama, Mississippi, and Louisiana. From 3,000 bales of cotton in 1790, the South was exporting 178,000 bales by the early part of the nineteenth century.[12] Cotton eventually became the most important export of the United States.

American merchants soon began to smuggle slaves into the United States, in violation of the state laws that banned the trade. South Carolina, which had out-lawed the trade, reopened the port of Charleston to legal slaving. Between 1787 and 1808, ninety thousand slaves were shipped into South Carolina.[13] The trade would still continue even after abolition by federal law.

During the 1800s, the United States entered a period of illegal slave trade. Merchants would now find themselves clashing repeatedly with federal law.

CHAPTER 5

THE SLAVE TRADE AND THE LAW

"**T**HE HARDSHIPS AND INCONVENIENCES suffered by the Negroes during the passage are scarcely to be enumerated or conceived," explained Dr. Alexander Falconbridge, who had served aboard an English slave ship. They were frequently stowed below deck, Falconbridge added.

> The confined air, rendered noxious . . . soon produces fevers and fluxes which generally carries off great numbers of them. . . . The deck, that is the floor of their rooms, was so covered with the blood and mucus which had proceeded from them in consequence of the flux, that it resembled a slaughter-house.[1]

As a result of testimony from Dr. Falconbridge and others, the British parliament voted to ban the slave trade throughout their empire in 1807. A majority of the English people had become convinced that, no matter how profitable the slave trade might be, it was immoral. That same year, the United States Congress also voted to end the slave trade. As President Thomas Jefferson, a slave owner himself, commented:

> I congratulate you, fellow-citizens . . . to withdraw . . . the United States from all further participation in those violations of human rights which have been so long continued on the unoffending inhabitants of Africa, and which the morality, the reputation, and the best interests of our country, have long been eager to proscribe [ban].[2]

The ban became effective in 1808. The new law called for a fine of twenty thousand dollars and loss of a slave ship to anyone convicted of equipping a slaver. A fine was also levied on anyone transporting and selling slaves. There was also a prison sentence of five to ten years.

Enforcing the Law
The British and Americans went about the task of enforcing the new laws against the slave trade quite differently. The English decided not only to stop the slave trade in their own empire, but in other empires, as well. The British navy was the most powerful in the world. Therefore, it had the strength to enforce the anti-slave-trade effort. In 1817, the Le Louis case had stated that the British could not search suspected slave ships flying the flags of foreign countries unless these nations agreed to allow the searches. That same year,

the British signed agreements with Portugal and Spain. These agreements allowed English naval ships to search Portuguese and Spanish vessels that might be carrying slaves. In addition, the Spanish and Portuguese agreed to stop the slave trade in their empires north of the equator. This did not affect colonies such as Brazil.

The British also signed agreements with African leaders along the west coast to end the slave trade. Over the half century between 1810 and 1860, the English captured an estimated 160,000 Africans

This illustration shows the capture of a slave ship called the *Medallion* in the Bay of Kabina, Africa.

headed to the New World and captured 1,600 slave ships.[3]

Unfortunately, this was only a small percentage of the number of slaves who reached the Americas. Because the demand for slaves was still very high on the sugar plantations of the Caribbean and South America, slavers were willing to risk being caught. Many traders sailed faster ships than the British could put on duty to patrol West Africa. Some contemporaries also believed that the English did not try as hard as possible to stop the trade. They thought that because English-made goods were used to trade with the Africans, the British ships sometimes looked the other way.[4]

The Spanish, meanwhile, disregarded the agreements they had made with the English. Spanish ships still carried slaves to the island of Cuba. The Spanish government was willing to permit the trade because slaves were necessary to work on the sugarcane plantations. The sugar industry brought in a lot of money in taxes for the empire. Slaves were also being carried to the Portuguese colony of Brazil. When Brazil became independent in 1822, the slave trade continued.

Slavers from the United States were deeply involved in the trade from Africa to the Caribbean and South America. As President James Madison commented in 1810, "[I]t appears that American citizens are instrumental in carrying on a traffic in enslaved Africans, equally in violation of the laws of humanity, and in defiance of those of their own country."[5] Ships built in harbors such as Baltimore, New York, and Bristol participated in the slave trade. These ships were often sold to slavers in other countries. They used the ships and the protection of the American flag to stop British naval vessels from stopping and searching them.

The United States refused to allow British ships to stop and search American vessels. In the past, British naval vessels had stopped American ships illegally. This had raised a huge protest among Americans because it violated their rights. During the nineteenth century, Spanish and Portuguese slavers routinely sailed under American flags. This enabled them to avoid search and seizure by the British.

American slavers themselves participated in the slave trade. American merchants not only brought slaves to the colonies of other countries, but also in some cases into the United States. In Louisiana, the pirate Jean Lafitte carried on a lucrative slave trade during the early part of the nineteenth century. Later, he moved his slave operations to Galveston, Texas, which was part of Spanish Mexico at the time. Slaves brought into this harbor were then smuggled into the

United States. Another port of entry was Amelia Island, off the coast of Florida. Florida was part of the Spanish empire until it was purchased in 1819 by the United States. Although Amelia Island was captured by U.S. troops in 1817, the slave trade continued. Slavers also continued to enter U.S. ports, such as Mobile, Alabama, and New Orleans, Louisiana. The United States government needed to send naval ships to halt the trade, but it was not willing to spend the money.

United States Laws Against the Slave Trade

Nevertheless, the United States government did take other measures to strengthen the laws against the slave trade. In 1818, a new law was passed, giving informers financial rewards if they told the government about slavers. The following year, Congress passed another law, which authorized President James Monroe to send ships to Africa and to patrol the American coast to stop U.S. slave traders. But the law was only weakly enforced. In 1819, New York congressman General James Tallmadge reported that about fourteen thousand slaves had illegally entered the United States over the previous year.[6] In 1820, another law made slave trading an act of piracy, punishable by death. But no slave trader would be prosecuted under the law for over forty years.

However, a few U.S. ships were sent to the African

coast to work with the British to control the slave trade. These ships were supposed to stop American vessels engaged in the trade. The Americans did capture several slavers, but the slavers claimed to be Spanish. Nevertheless, the papers on their vessels indicated that they might be owned by Americans. As far as the American navy was concerned, however, this evidence was not conclusive. Because the United States would not allow anyone to search its ships, the American vessels had to let the Spanish slavers return to the high seas. Many American ships pretended to be Spanish to escape capture. The United States naval vessels stopped so few ships that the patrol was removed from the African coast.

The slavers eluded the American patrol ships, and resorted to similar tactics to elude the British patrols. Spanish slave traders, for example, would fly American flags because these ships could not be searched by the British navy. According to one estimate quoted by historian Warren Howard, "99 percent of all 'American' vessels in the business were actually owned by foreigners."[7] Slavers also used a variety of other strategies to avoid patrols. For example, they would land some of their crew to do business with African traders, then put out to sea to avoid patrols along the coast. Slave ships had to carry food and water to feed the slaves who came aboard. However, if the ships were approached by a patrol, they would claim that the food was to be used in legitimate trade with Africans. The water was labeled "wine," which was used in the African trade. Wood was put on board to build another deck below the top deck and above the ship's hold for stowing the slaves. The slavers claimed that the wood was simply used in legitimate trade.[8]

Many U.S. slavers were very successful in continuing their trade along the African coast. However, they were no longer bringing the slaves to the United States for the most part. Most of these slaves were brought to the Caribbean and South America. A report to the American Secretary of the Navy reported that ships out of Baltimore, Charleston, and New Orleans were involved in the trade.

However, the British still succeeded in capturing some slave ships. During 1839, the British ship *Buzzard* brought two American slavers into New York harbor. Other slavers were escorted into New York by a British naval vessel a short time later. The owners were expected to be tried in an American court for violating the slave trade laws. The U.S. government contended, however, that it was not clear that two of the ships were owned by Americans. They appeared to be owned by Spaniards. Therefore, the ships were released. The other ships clearly seemed to have American owners. One of the ships was confiscated because slaves had been on board. The other was not. It had no slaves at the time of its capture. However, material on board made it obvious that the ship was involved in the slave trade.

During the nineteenth century, slavery was a heated issue in the United States. Southerners believed it was their right to keep slaves. They were also prepared to look the other way when it came to the illegal slave trade. In the North, some Americans called abolitionists wanted to see an immediate end to slavery. But they were considered radicals. The majority of northerners were prepared to let the South keep the institution of slavery. After all, cotton grown on southern plantations was used in northern textile mills to make cloth. These mills provided jobs for thousands of northern workers.

The *Amistad* Case

One of the most publicized cases regarding the slave trade involved the slave ship, *Amistad*. It was captured off the coast of New York in 1839. The *Amistad* was carrying slaves from Cuba. These slaves had been brought onto the island from Africa, in violation of Spanish law ending the slave trade. The slaves were purchased in Havana and put aboard the *Amistad*. They were to be taken along the Cuban coast to a plantation. Along the way, the slaves mutinied. Led by an

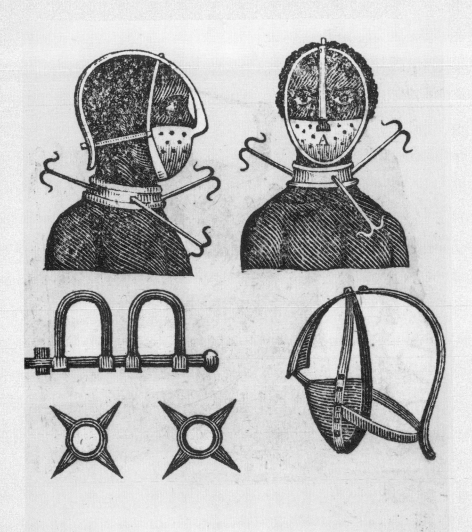

Slave traders used various ways to restrain slaves as they were transported from one place to another.

African named Cinqué, they overwhelmed the small crew and killed some of them. The Africans then took control of the ship. They had hoped to sail back to Africa. However, the remaining members of the crew would sail toward North America at night when they were less likely to be caught by the Africans. The *Amistad* was captured by a U.S. naval vessel near New York, and the Africans put into prison.

Because the Africans had committed murder and taken over a Spanish ship, the government of Spain wanted them returned to Cuba. The Spanish argued that the Africans were slaves and the property of Spanish citizens. President Martin Van Buren agreed. However, when the Africans were brought to trial, a district judge disagreed. Early in 1840, he had ruled that the Africans were not slaves. They had been captured illegally. Therefore, as free men, they had a right to protect their freedom by taking control of the *Amistad*. The judge ruled that they should be set free.

At this point, President Van Buren decided to take the case to the Supreme Court. Van Buren was running for reelection. He needed the votes of southern states to achieve victory. Many southerners were angry about the verdict in the *Amistad* case. They believed that it gave slaves the right to rebel. The case was argued before the Supreme Court by John Quincy Adams. Formerly president of the United States and at that time a congressman from Massachusetts, Adams was a strong opponent of slavery. In March 1841, the Supreme Court ruled that the Africans were not slaves and should be freed. The case was a clear victory against the slave trade.

The Slave Trade in the 1840s and 1850s

Nevertheless, an illegal American slave trade continued. In 1842, Great Britain and the United States signed the Webster-Ashburton Treaty. This called for American ships to be sent back to the African coast. They were expected to work together with the British navy to shut down the slave trade. However, the U.S. government sent only two ships in 1843. These ships could not patrol the long African coastline and detect American ships engaged in the slave trade alone. In addition, slavers continued to use various strategies to avoid capture. As historian W.E.B. Du Bois wrote: "The *Illinois* of Gloucester, Massachusetts, while lying at Whydah, Africa, was boarded by a British officer, but having American papers was unmolested. Three days later she hoisted Spanish colors and sailed away with a cargo of slaves."[9]

Over the next ten years, however, the U.S. squadron took very few slavers. As a result, little was done to prevent American captains from participating in the slave trade. American slave traders sailed out of

New Orleans; Havana, Cuba; and New York. They continued to transport slaves to Cuba and Brazil.

Meanwhile, several important legal cases highlighted the attitudes toward the slave trade in the United States. In 1856, Rudolph E. Lasala was tried for owning a vessel that he knew was involved in the slave trade. It was clear that he was guilty. Under the federal law of 1818, he could be sent to prison. However, the judge in the case, Samuel R. Betts, put an unusual interpretation on the 1818 law. He said that Lasala could only be found guilty if he was in charge of the ship during its voyage to Africa. Because he was not the captain, the jury was forced to find him not guilty. Judge Betts had taken the power out of the 1818 law.

In 1858, the slave ship *Echo* was captured along with 318 slaves and brought into Charleston harbor. When the crew came up for trial, however, the jury refused to regard them in violation of the law. At the same time, according to historian Warren Howard, the South reported that the "community is strongly opposed to the execution of the laws prohibiting the slave trade. . . ."[10] The *Echo* case supported the position taken by many people in the South. Southerners feared that the institution of slavery was in jeopardy. More and more voices in the North were denouncing slavery as evil and immoral. Southerners were opposed to any laws that might restrict what they saw

Most of the slave trade operated out of the African Gold Coast.

as their right to uphold the institution of slavery. This seemed to include the freedom to engage in the illegal slave trade.

A year later, an incident arose involving the ship *Wanderer.* It secretly landed three to four hundred slaves on the Georgia coast. The ship could not sail directly into Savannah, Georgia, which was guarded by a fort. Instead, an observer reported, the captain

> crept into the mouth of the Great Ogeechee [river], by night, and ascended the river to the big swamp and there lay concealed while he communicated with Charles L.A.

Lamar, his Savannah owner. Lamar thereupon announced that he was going to give a grand ball in honor of the officers and garrison of the fort, and insisted that the soldiers, as well as their superiors, should partake of the good cheer. When the gayety was at its height, the *Wanderer* stole into the river and passed the guns of the fort unchallenged in the darkness and made her way to Lamar's plantations, some distance up the river.[11]

Later, the incident was discovered, but the government could do nothing. Some of the people involved in slave trading were arrested. However, nothing could be proved.

Several thousand slaves continued to be imported into Georgia and elsewhere until the early 1860s. The demand for slaves continued, as plantations expanded, and prices kept going up. A slave who sold for $550 to $625 in 1846 was selling for $1,500 to $1,625 in 1860.[12] Reports from Mobile, Alabama; Vicksburg, Mississippi; and Memphis, Tennessee, told of slaves from Africa being sold in these cities. Nevertheless, the numbers of slaves from Africa were relatively small. Most slaves were being transported throughout the South itself. Indeed, the internal slave trade became the primary means by which slaves reached the new plantations.

SLAVE TRADE
WITHIN THE SOUTH

DURING THE NINETEENTH CENTURY, important changes occurred in the nature of southern slavery. First, the number of slaves increased enormously. The United States census of 1790 showed that approximately 670,000 slaves lived in the South. Almost one-half of these slaves, 396,000, could be found in Virginia and Maryland.[1] By 1860, the slave population had reached almost 4 million.[2] Now, about 60 percent of these slaves could be found in the states of Alabama, Arkansas, Florida, Louisiana, Mississippi, and Texas.[3] The number of slaves in Maryland had declined.

Since 1808, federal law had banned the importation of slaves from Africa. Although some slaves were smuggled into the United States illegally, they do not account for the tremendous increase in the slave population. That increase was primarily due to natural causes. That is, slaves had children. During the nineteenth century, there was also a vast movement of slaves from the Old South to the states of the deep South. Most of these states were formed out of the area that had been part of the Louisiana Purchase. This was a vast territory of over eight hundred thousand square miles acquired by President Thomas Jefferson from France in 1803. Carved out of part of this area were the states of Alabama, Louisiana, and Mississippi. Florida was acquired from Spain in 1819, becoming a state in 1845. That same year, Texas also entered the Union.

All these states in the South had a climate that was suitable for growing cotton. Plantations were rapidly carved out from cheap land by settlers coming from other parts of the South. The production of cotton grew very fast. From 178,000 bales produced in 1810, the South was producing 4 million bales by 1860.[4] Much of the cotton went to Great Britain. British cotton mills turned the raw cotton into cloth for clothing and other items. Part of the cotton was also shipped north to the mills of New England. In states such as Massachusetts, there was a thriving textile manufacturing industry. This industry depended on raw cotton grown on southern plantations.

To produce the cotton, plantation owners

SOURCE DOCUMENT

TO BE SOLD, on board the
Ship *Bance-Ifland*, on tuefday the 6th
of *May* next, at *Afhley-Ferry*; a choice
cargo of about 250 fine healthy

NEGROES,

juft arrived from the
Windward & Rice Coaft.
—The utmoft care has
already been taken, and
fhall be continued, to keep them free from
the leaft danger of being infected with the
SMALL-POX, no boat having been on
board, and all other communication with
people from *Charles-Town* prevented.

Auftin, Laurens, & Appleby.

N. B. Full one Half of the above Negroes have had the
SMALL-POX in their own Country.

Slaves were often advertised in the classifieds of newspapers. The
author of this ad emphasizes that these particular slaves were kept
away from the dangers of smallpox. This disease had plagued the
American Indians when European settlers first arrived.

depended on a steady supply of labor to work their land. This was provided by African-American slaves.

The Slave Migration

The slave migration had already begun during the late eighteenth century. The indigo plantations had disappeared as a result of the American Revolution. England no longer wanted indigo from the United States. In addition, tobacco declined in Virginia and Maryland. Growing tobacco exhausted the soil of the plantations. Therefore, in a state like Virginia, the size of the tobacco crops had decreased. Plantation owners such as Thomas Jefferson found themselves in debt. In fact, Jefferson sold some of his slaves to pay his creditors. Other plantation owners found that they no longer needed as many slaves as they had in the past. Therefore, they were willing to sell them to new plantations springing up in other parts of the South.

Most of the sales were made indirectly. Instead, slave traders bought slaves from plantation owners in Virginia, Maryland, and South Carolina. Then, the traders transported them westward and sold them to new owners. Advertisements in local newspapers, placed by plantation owners in Virginia, indicated that some of their slaves were for sale. Typical advertisements stated, a valuable negro fellow, about 28 years old, who knew something of carpentry. . . .

two valuable young men, one an excellent shoemaker and the other a nailor, in which a great bargain might be realized. . . .

for sale several . . . Negro Girls, From twelve to eighteen years of age, for Cash.[5]

Slave traders also advertised for slaves. One advertisement in Maryland read: "150 SERVANTS WANTED—of all descriptions—mechanics of all kinds from 12 to twenty-five years of age; also 50 in families; it is desirable to purchase them in large lots as they will be settled in Alabama. . . ."[6]

In addition to advertising, slave traders would also let it be known by word of mouth that they were looking for slaves. They might go to the local tavern or general store and talk to townspeople to find out if anyone had slaves that might be for sale. Much of the slave trade occurred in the countryside, although trading also took place in major cities like Richmond, Virginia, or Baltimore, Maryland.

Historian Ira Berlin has called this new movement of slaves the Second Middle Passage. He estimates, that from 1810 to 1820, 120,000 slaves were being transported. Three hundred thousand slaves were moved during the 1830s, with about one third of them going to Alabama and Mississippi.[7] Historians believe that as many as one million slaves were moved from one plantation to another by the domestic slave trade.[8] The slaves were sold from states like Virginia, Maryland, and the Carolinas to states in the deep South. These included Louisiana, Mississippi, Alabama, Arkansas, and Texas. Some of these slaves went with their masters, who may have left one plantation and relocated somewhere else. Some owners went west and established cotton plantations, which they hoped would be more profitable than old tobacco plantations. The majority of slaves, however, were sold by plantation owners to the slave traders.

The Slave Traders
Internal slave trade within the South was completely legal. Slave traders set up business in every important city. In Maryland, for example, part of the slave trade was carried out in Baltimore. This was also a center of the illegal slave trade to Africa.

One of the best-known slave traders was Austin Woolfolk, whose family was engaged in the slave trade for many years. In 1826, Woolfolk loaded a consignment of slaves aboard his ship *Decatur*. They staged a mutiny, however, and took over the ship. But the ship was eventually recaptured. Woolfolk was willing to take his chances with occasional mutinies. The prices for slaves were high, and the profits could be large.

Other well-known slave traders in the east included Franklin & Armfield of Alexandria, Virginia. Their agents operated in cities such as Richmond and Baltimore. Richmond, in fact, had eighteen people who listed themselves as slave traders. Some slave traders collected slaves from plantations in the countryside, then brought them to Richmond. Here they were sold to other traders who took them into the deep South. Slave traders who did a brisk business there included Thomas A. Powell & Company of Montgomery, Alabama; Matthews, Branton & Company of Natchez, Mississippi; and B. M. Campbell of New Orleans, Louisiana.

Slave trading was essential to the new plantations that arose in the South. Many white southerners saw nothing wrong with employing slaves. However, they often professed to look down on slave traders. Because they made their living buying and selling human beings, their work was considered contemptible. Slave traders also had a reputation for abusing some of their slaves.

In his book *Speculators and Slaves*, historian Michael Tadman explained that the public image of slave traders did not really match reality. Some slave traders became very wealthy and held respectable positions in their communities. As Tadman pointed out, they held political office and became directors of

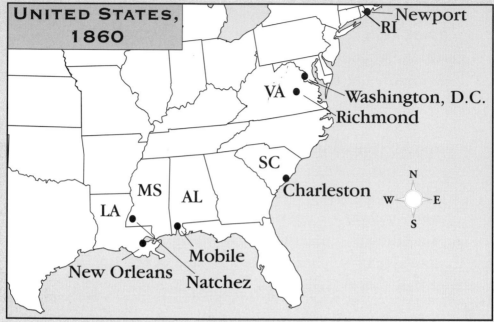

By 1860, many American cities had operated as slave trading centers.

local banks. In Charleston, one of the most prominent families was the Gadsdens. Although Thomas Gadsden was a slave trader, his "close relatives included a bishop and a prominent lawyer," as well as a respected diplomat.[9]

Slaves Born to Slaves

During the nineteenth century, the abolitionists in the North accused the slave owners of raising slaves to sell them and make large profits. Historians believe that the abolitionists—who wanted to see slavery ended— had overstated the situation in the South. After all, African-American slaves were essential to the running of plantations. Nevertheless, plantation owners never lost sight of the fact that slaves were an important form of wealth. In states such as Virginia, the sale of tobacco and the sale of slaves were the best methods of earning money for the plantation owners.

During the middle of the nineteenth century, the landscape architect Frederick Law Olmsted, who later designed Central Park in New York City, traveled to the South. Olmsted recalled a conversation with one slave owner who was praising his female slaves for producing so many babies. The slave owner said

> his women were uncommonly good breeders; he did not suppose there was a lot of women anywhere that bred faster than his; he never heard of babies coming so fast as they did on his plantation; it was perfectly surprising; and every one of them, in his estimation, was worth two hundred dollars, as negroes were selling now, the moment it drew breath.[10]

Historians have also noted instances where slave women were given rewards by their masters for having children. Some slaves were even offered their freedom if they produced a specified number of offspring.[11] However, historian Michael Tadman points out that there is no evidence for slave breeding in the South. Slave babies, he explains, were not being sold by planters and traders. In addition, the slaves had a strong sense of family. These families would not have been possible if slaves believed that their babies would be sold soon after they were born.[12]

Separating Families

Many slaves were moved between plantations and between states. During the 1850s, for example, slaves from Delaware, Maryland, Virginia, and the Carolinas supplied over 60 percent of those being transported. And about 90 percent of them were moved to the states of the deep South—Mississippi, Louisiana, Arkansas, and Texas.[13] Historians have investigated whether these slaves were sold with their families or whether the families were separated.

According to a study done of slavery in Maryland, almost 30 percent of slave unions, or marriages, were destroyed by the slave trade.[14] Other estimates put the number of slave marriages that were broken up at about 20 percent.[15] One of the most troubling aspects of the slave trade was separating African-American families. Some states had laws that prevented children under the age of eight or ten from being sold away from their mothers. But these laws were rarely

Mother and child were often sold away from one another. Some slaves never saw their families again. Others ran away with their families in order to stay together.

enforced. Most states had no laws regarding the sale of slave children.

Some slaves recalled being sent off by their masters to do some work. When they came back, their wives and children might have been sold, never to be seen again. As historian Michael Tadman wrote:

Another slave put on her best clothes and joyfully accompanied her master, who had told her that her free papers [setting her free] were at last to be completed if she went with him. The paper signed by the master was, however, a bill of sale: the result was delivery to a trader and separation from her family.[16]

Another observer who traveled in the South, Professor Ethan Andrews, wrote about the following conversation he had with a slave trader. When asking whether he bought an entire family, the trader answered that he regularly purchased the wife alone and that "frequently . . . they sell me the mother while they keep the children. I have often known them [to] take away the infant from its mother's breast and keep it, while they sold her." When asked how this made the mothers feel, Andrews was told that "they take on *right smart* [grieve], for a long time."[17]

One slave recalled being purchased when he was ten years old. This involved a painful separation from his mother.

> I looked round and saw my poor mother stretching out her hands after me. She ran up, and overtook us, but [my new master] . . . would not let her approach, though she begged and prayed to be allowed to kiss me for the last time, and bid me good bye. I was so stupified with grief and fright, that I could not shed a tear, thought my heart was bursting. . . . That was the last time I ever saw her. . . .[18]

Young children were not widely prized by slave traders or plantation owners. They were more mouths to feed, while being unable to do any work. Of course, some plantation owners were not so hard-hearted. They tried to keep slave families together. If forced to sell them because of financial hard times, they made every effort to sell entire families together. But other owners were not so considerate; they would do whatever the slave traders wanted. This might mean selling the members of slave families separately. Sometimes, slave children were also sent from one plantation to another as gifts. These might be given by a planter to a member of his family who had moved away or to his married daughter to celebrate the birth of a child.

How did the white plantation owners justify separating African-American families? As historian Michael Tadman has written, the southern plantation owners believed that they should determine what was best for black people. This was based on racism. The plantation owners reasoned that black families were not stable. "Blacks were seen as permanent children, or worse. They might have sometimes 'excitable' attachments to family, but essentially such feelings were seen as short-lived."[19] Plantation owners believed that they must decide what was in the best interests of running their plantations. They should also determine where blacks could be best employed, because these slaves did not have the ability to do it for themselves. If that meant selling them to another plantation, then it must be done.[20]

SOURCE DOCUMENT

I would much rather you would get married to some good man, for every time I gits a letter from you it tears me all to pieces. The reason why I have not written you before, in a long time, is because your letters disturbed me so very much. You know I love my children. I treats them good as a Father can treat his children; and I do a good deal of it for you. I was sorry to hear that Lewellyn, my poor little son, have had such bad health. I would come and see you, but I know you could not bear it. I want to see you and I don't want to see you. I love you just as well as I did the last day I saw you, and it will not do for you and I to meet. I am married, and my wife have two children, and if you and I meets it would make a very dissatisfied family.[21]

Laura Spicer was sold away from her husband. He remarried because he thought she was dead. However, after the Civil War, she located him and they started to correspond. This is an excerpt from a letter to Laura Spicer from her husband.

Transporting Slaves

Slaves who reached the shores of North America from Africa always came by ship. But they traveled throughout the South by a variety of means. Some went by ship along the coast. They might be loaded on a vessel in Baltimore, Maryland; Norfolk, Virginia; or Charleston, South Carolina, and taken to the Gulf States. Often, the men and women were loaded into different compartments for the trip. The voyages, however, were not always smooth. Storms could sink a slave vessel or blow it off course.

Slaves also traveled by water on the steamboats that sailed up and down the Mississippi River. Slaves might be shipped from Memphis, Tennessee, or Vicksburg, Mississippi, to New Orleans, Louisiana. Usually, they were kept in chains to prevent their escape.

Many slaves traveled overland from the plantations in the east to the deep South. Here they were often roped together in long lines, called coffles. The men might wear iron collars, while the women were roped by their necks. They were accompanied by the slave traders, who carried guns and whips to keep the slaves moving along to their destinations. Often, they traveled at the rate of twenty-five miles per day until they reached the city where they were to be sold. Along the way, the slaves in the coffles sang. This would help them take their minds off their situation.

One observer described the coffle as a "funeral." Slaves were saddened to leave homes and families behind. Some could not stand the separation. They committed suicide. Others escaped and tried to leave the South forever.[22]

Another method of travel was the railroad. Frederick Olmsted wrote about being aboard a train with "two first-class passenger cars, and two freight cars. The latter were occupied by about forty negroes, most of them belonging to traders, who were sending them to the cotton States to be sold. Such kind of evidence of activity in the slave trade of Virginia is to be seen every day."[23]

Slaves traveled from Petersburg, Virginia, a major rail center, to the deep South. Others came from Augusta, Georgia, to Montgomery and Mobile, Alabama.

Cities like Montgomery, along with Charleston, Richmond, and New Orleans were the largest slave centers in the South. There, thousands of slaves were routinely bought and sold.

MAJOR CENTERS
OF INTERNAL
SLAVE TRADE

A SLAVE NAMED WILLIAM BROWN RECALLED the procedure for preparing slaves to be sold in the New Orleans slave market. As the slaves came down the Mississippi River, he was ordered to make the older slaves look younger so they would be more likely to be sold.

> I was ordered to have the old men's whiskers shaved off, and the grey hairs plucked out where they were not too numerous, in which case we had a preparation of blacking to color it, and with a blacking brush we put it on. . . . and I am sure that some of those who purchased slaves . . . were dreadfully cheated, especially in the ages of the slaves which they bought.[1]

New Orleans was the largest slave-trading center of the South. Generally, slaves were gathered by traders in the upper South during the summer. A slave trader named John Hagan, for example, purchased slaves in South Carolina and Virginia during the summer. Then, he took them to New Orleans in the fall.[2] The primary slave-selling season was January to March. This was after the harvest, when planters had sold their crops and had money to buy slaves. Unlike in other parts of the South, where the primary crop was cotton, many New Orleans slaves were bought to work in the sugar-cane fields. This was especially backbreaking work. Slaves often lasted only a few years before they died.[3]

Once slaves arrived in the city, they were housed in slave pens or jails. Large traders like Franklin & Armfield maintained pens in New Orleans. Slaves were bought in Virginia. Then, they might be held in a Franklin & Armfield pen in Alexandria. Eventually, they were shipped to New Orleans, often by one of the boats owned by the Franklin & Armfield firm. In a New Orleans pen, the slaves were given plenty of food to eat and dressed relatively well. The traders wanted to make sure that their slaves looked as good as possible so they would be purchased by the planters.

Slaves were generally sold in what was called private sales. That is, planters would come in to a trader's showroom near the pen. Then, they looked at the slaves and made their purchases from the traders.

Slave-trading companies maintained slave pens throughout the American South. The slave pen pictured was owned by Price, Birch, & Co. and was located in Alexandria, Virginia.

Before being offered for sale, the slaves were carefully instructed on how to present themselves.

As slave John Brown recalled:

> A man or a woman may be well made, and physically faultless in every respect, yet their value be impaired by a sour look, or a dull, vacant stare, or a general dulness [sic] of demeanor. For this reason the poor wretches who are about to be sold, are instructed to look "spry and smart:" to hold themselves well up, and put on a smiling, cheerful countenance.[4]

According to Brown, the slaves were separated according to size: "those who were nearly of the same height and make being put into separate lots . . . the various members of a family were of necessity separated, and would often see the last of one another in that dreadful show-room."[5]

The slaves were then carefully examined by prospective buyers, who often felt their limbs and looked in their mouths to inspect their teeth. Brown described what was expected of the slaves: "They must answer every question, and do as they are bid, to show themselves off; dance, jump, walk, leap, squat, tumble, and twist about, that the buyer may see they have no stiff joints, or other physical defect."[6]

Those who did not do as they were ordered might afterward be beaten with a "flopping paddle." Brown said the slaves were then

> stripped stark naked, and laid flat on the floor, with their face downwards. . . . The punishment is dreadfully severe, for all no blood is drawn. "Flopping" was inflicted for various offences, especially the unpardonable one of "not speaking up and looking bright and smart" when the buyers were choosing.[7]

The paddle, unlike a whip, showed no marks that might make it harder to sell a slave. A slave with whip marks indicated that he was high-spirited and rebellious. Such a slave would not be a calm and obedient worker.

Although slaves were generally sold in private sales by the traders, some slaves were also auctioned off in New Orleans. Among the well-known auctioneers were Joseph A. Beard and Julian Neville. Many slaves were auctioned off in the St. Charles Hotel in New Orleans. Another auction site was the St. Louis Hotel. This was a glamorous setting that attracted many people who came to see the auction. The slaves were displayed under a magnificent domed ceiling. The auctioneer called on participants to bid on men, women, and children. Auctions were held on Saturdays and became popular social events. At the auction, a trader frequently provided planters with a catalogue or price list. Each slave was given a number and described. For example, the best workers would be called "No. 1 Men" or "No. 1 Girls." Those of lower quality might be called "Second Rate or Ordinary Men," or "Second Rate or Ordinary Girls." In this

Here, a prospective buyer in North Africa checks the health of an enslaved African by examining his teeth. This practice was continued in nineteenth-century America.

way, buyers and sellers had some idea of the quality of each slave. Then, they could reach agreement on a satisfactory price.

One slave trader named John White worked in New Orleans for approximately twenty years. His account books showed the prices for which he bought and sold some of his slaves:

Isabel Evans, 17, $600.00   Sold to Mr. Herne, cash $750.00

William Robards, 25, $750.00   Sold to C. H. Harriss, N. Orleans, $875.00

Joe Fields, 22, $715.00   Sold to Etienne Landry, Lafourche, cash $800.00[8]

Of course, these figures did not indicate pure profit. There was the cost of shipping the slaves to market. A trader had to provide food on the journey. He also had to pay for the chains and ropes to bind the slaves. In New Orleans, there was the cost of keeping slaves in a pen, which might run to twenty-five or thirty cents per day. In addition, the trader had to pay for clothes and might even provide a doctor to examine the slaves for illness. None of these things were done for the benefit of the slaves. They were designed to make sure that a trader could get the highest price when he sold them.

Montgomery, Mobile, and Natchez

Eastward from New Orleans were smaller slave markets in Alabama and Mississippi. Montgomery, Alabama, for example, had four locations were slaves were sold. These slaves came from states such as Virginia and South Carolina. Another center of the slave trade was Mobile, Alabama, north of Montgomery. Here slaves were auctioned by Belthazer Tardy & Company. The auctioneers wanted the slaves they sold to be in good condition so they could get the highest price for them. One slave from Mobile named Joseph Holmes was interviewed during the 1930s at the age of 81. He explained that the planter who owned his plantation never mistreated his slaves because he was raising them for market, and it would not be good business to mistreat them.[9]

A third slave-trading city was Natchez, Mississippi, located on the Mississippi River. Slaves from the Carolinas and Kentucky were often transported to pens run by Natchez traders and sold to planters.

A visitor to the Natchez slave market recalled seeing planters as well as ladies coming to the pens to buy slaves. One woman, he said,

> purchased two, a young mother and her child, and in a few minutes afterward, at the solicitation [request] of the youth, purchased the husband of the girl, and all three, with happy faces—happier, that they were not to be

SOURCE DOCUMENT

Having rapidly sketched these features, I had not time to put my outline away before a whole group of buyers and dealers were in the compartment. . . . The auctioneer, who had mounted his table, came down and asked me whether, "if I had a business store, and someone came in and interrupted my trading, I should like it." This was unanswerable; I got up with the intention of leaving quietly, but, feeling this would savour of flight, I turned round to the now evidently angry crowd of dealers, and said, "You may turn me away, but I can recollect all I have seen."[10]

Eyre Crowe, secretary to British writer William Makepeace Thackeray, wrote an account of a slave auction in Richmond, Virginia, in 1853.

separated—flew to get their little parcels, and rode away with their mistress. . . .[11]

Savannah and Charleston

The largest slave trader in Savannah, Georgia, was Joseph Bryan. He sold large gangs of slaves, sometimes over 450. They were advertised throughout the South so many buyers would arrive and bid up the prices of the slaves. With so many slaves to sell, Bryan even had a catalogue. Each slave was briefly described and given a number so the buyers could distinguish one slave from another. Such a large group of slaves required Bryan to hold the sale at a nearby horse-racing course. The slaves waited in the grandstands. Then, one by one, they were led into a room and sold over two days in 1859.

A much larger slave-trading center than Savannah was Charleston. In front of the customhouse in Charleston, thousands of slaves were sold each year at auctions. Slaves often came from other parts of South Carolina. In 1857, a No. 1 Man was being sold for between $1,250 and $1,450. That is the equivalent of about $21,000 to $24,000 today. A No. 1 Girl sold for between $1,050 and $1,225. That is the equivalent of about $17,500 to $20,500 today.[12]

The Richmond Market

Richmond, Virginia, was one of the most successful slave markets in the South. Traders often bought slaves in the countryside around Richmond. Then, the slaves were brought in to slave pens. One of these pens was run by Bob Lumpkin. As one contemporary observer described the pen,

> On one side of the court [was] . . . a large open tank for washing. . . . Opposite was a long, two-story brick house, the lower part fitted up for men and the second story for

women. The place, in fact, was a kind of hotel or board-inghouse for negro traders and their slaves.[13]

After the slaves were fed and properly clothed, they might be sold privately at a pen. Those who were not sold were taken to large halls and auctioned off. The auctioneers took about a 2 to 3 percent commission. The buyers were usually other traders who took the slaves to New Orleans and elsewhere.[14]

One contemporary account describes the sale of a slave who was crying when she was sold. When asked why, she said, "'Because I have left my man behind, and his master won't let him come along.' [The trader

Slaves were put on public display at auctions, while slave buyers shouted out bids. It was a humiliating experience that often ended in the slave being separated from his or her family.

answered:] 'Oh, if I buy you, I will furnish you with a better husband, or man as you call him, than your old one.' 'I don't want any *better* and won't have any *other* as long as he lives.'"[15]

The Washington, D.C., Market

For many years, a busy slave market existed in Washington. This was the site of the capitol of the United States. There was not a large number of slaves in the District of Columbia itself. But slaves were sold there from Maryland and northern Virginia to work on plantations farther south. Among the most prominent slave traders was J. W. Neal & Company. This firm maintained a slave pen in the District. Another slave pen was owned by James H. Burch. He was described by a slave named Solomon Northrup as "a man whose whole appearance was sinister and repugnant."[16] He sold slaves to the markets in New Orleans. Northrup was kept in the pen before being sold. He was imprisoned in a room

about twelve feet square—the walls of solid masonry. . . . There was one small window, crossed with great iron bars, with an outside shutter, securely fastened. . . . The furniture of the room in which I was, consisted of the wooden bench on which I sat, an old-fashioned dirty box stove, and besides these, in either cell, there was neither bed, nor blanket, nor any other thing whatever.[17]

Northrup was severely beaten by Burch, who used a paddle on him that would not show the marks. "Blow after blow was inflicted upon my naked body. . . . At length the paddle broke, leaving the useless handle in his hand. . . ."[18]

Slave trade continued in the District of Columbia until 1850, when it was outlawed by new legislation. The legislation was part of the so-called Compromise of 1850, passed by the United States Senate and approved by President Millard Filmore. The compromise had been necessary to prevent a secession by some of the southern states. These states felt threatened by increasing opposition to slavery in the North. Southerners wanted to extend slavery into the new western territories. These territories had been acquired from Mexico as a result of the United States victory in the Mexican War, fought from 1846 to 1848. Many northerners did not want to see slavery extended into these territories. According to the Compromise of 1850, settlers in the new territories of New Mexico and Utah would decide for themselves whether to admit slavery. California would be admitted as a free state. Northerners would have to follow a stricter runaway-slave law. As part of the compromise, slavery was permitted to continue in the District of Columbia. However, the slave trade was banned.

The 1850s

The Compromise of 1850 may have put off war for another ten years. However, many northerners continued to decry the evils of slavery. In the South, meanwhile, planters defended the institution. The slave trade continued. Vigorous markets in slave trading existed throughout the South during the 1850s. In fact, historians have shown that slave prices continued to increase. In Richmond, for example, prices reached

The slave trade thrived in the capital of the United States until it was banned as part of the Compromise of 1850.

their height in 1860. A prime field hand might be selling for over \$1,600.[19] Clearly, the demand for slaves to work the plantations had not ended. During the 1850s, the price of cotton was rising. Many people in the South also believed that slaves were an excellent investment. This belief drove the prices of slaves even higher.

During the nineteenth century, slave owners often tried to defend the institution of slavery. They claimed that slaves were as well treated as factory workers in major cities. These employees often worked for long hours at low pay and lived in dismal poverty. But the factory employee could not be sold by his employer. The threat of being sold was always held over the head of a slave by his master. As former slave George Johnson put it, "If a man did anything out of the way he was in more danger of being sold than being whipped."[20] Another slave added, "I had a constant dread that Mrs. Moore [the slave's owner] would be in want of money and sell my dear wife. We constantly dreaded a final separation.[21]

As one slave, Fountain Hughes, said, "They'd sell us like they sell horses an' cows an' hogs an' all like that."[22]

This sense of being treated like an animal was reinforced during the sale or the auction itself. Buyers would examine a slave, who was often asked to strip naked. The slave was questioned to ensure that he was healthy. Then, he was asked to explain what types of work he could do. Finally, a buyer and trader might haggle over the price for the slave. It was a humiliating experience.

But this was simply part of the lives of African-American slaves in the South. They could be bought and sold at will. However, slaves sometimes did things to look less desirable to a buyer, like acting listless and tired.

Slave trading was an important part of the southern economy. In 1840, for example, the value of the crops sold by the South was placed at approximately $32 million. The value of the slaves reached over $6 million, or nearly 20 percent of the total. Over the next twenty years, the value of slaves being sold would reach over $9 million.[23]

However, these days were numbered. The beginning of the Civil War would change slavery and the slave trade forever.

END OF THE SLAVE TRADE

EARLY IN 1860, THE SAILING SHIP *THOMAS Watson* left the harbor at New London, Connecticut. The ship was supposedly setting out on an expedition to hunt whales. The oil and wax from sperm whales was used to lubricate machinery and make soap. In fact, the whaling industry was among the most important businesses in New England. But, as it turned out, whaling was not the actual purpose of the *Thomas Watson*. Instead, the ship was headed for the west coast of Africa. There the captain hoped to pick up a large supply of slaves. The *Thomas Watson* was involved in the illegal slave trade.

After reaching the coast of Africa, men, women, and children were brought out to the ship in boats. Then, they were stowed below decks. Edward Manning was one of the crewmen. When he signed on to serve aboard the *Thomas Watson*, Manning had not been told that the ship was a slaver. As Manning recalled,

> The Negroes had been put into the hold without the least regard for stowage. Consequently, they were literally piled on one another; and the unsteady motion of the ship, combined with the foul air and great heat, made the place simply horrible. Naturally they were nearly all dreadfully sick at the stomach. . . . Pent up in such close quarters and inhaling such a terrible stench, it was miraculous that one-half of them had not perished. We found five or six dead bodies which were at once hoisted to the deck and consigned to the deep.[1]

Over eight hundred Africans had been loaded aboard the *Thomas Watson*. As the ship proceeded across the Atlantic Ocean, diseases broke out among the slaves. Eventually, the ship reached its destination—Cuba. Schooners met the *Thomas Watson* to take the slaves secretly to shore. Slave trading was at this time illegal in Cuba.

Meanwhile, the captain had been paid with a large suitcase filled with coins. The ship then left and sailed for Mexico. From here, Manning headed north and arrived in New Orleans in January 1861.

Secession and the Slave Trade

When Manning returned to the United States, he found the nation in the midst of a grave crisis. In November 1860, Republican Abraham Lincoln had been elected President. Some slaveholders and their allies feared that Lincoln would not only prevent the extension of slavery, but try to abolish it throughout the United States. In December, southern slaveholding states began to secede from the Union. In February 1861, they established a new government, called the Confederate States of America.

The constitution of the new government read in part: "The importation of negroes of the African race, from any foreign country other than the slaveholding States or Territories of the United States, is hereby forbidden; and Congress is required to pass such laws as shall effectually prevent the same."[2]

The Confederacy had decided to outlaw the international slave trade, but not because it did not support the trade. Indeed, southern radicals had wanted to reopen the African slave trade during the 1850s. This would have made more slaves available to southerners. One reason the Confederacy outlawed the international slave trade was concern about it in Great Britain. The British were strong opponents of the slave trade. The Confederate leaders wanted British support in their coming conflict against the North. These leaders also wanted the support of the American border states, like Missouri and Kentucky. Here opinion was divided over whether to support the Confederacy or the Union. Therefore, Confederate leaders decided to include a statement in their constitution outlawing the African slave trade. However, the constitution of the Confederacy did not prevent individual southern states from importing slaves.[3]

Meanwhile, the northern government made a much stronger effort to end the African trade. In 1861, Congress voted the enormous sum of $1.8 million to halt the slave trade. Federal officials were ordered to search any ships, which might be slavers, leaving northern harbors. U.S. patrol ships sailed along the coast of Africa. Suspected slave ships were stopped. One slave captain, Nathaniel Gordon of the *Erie*, was imprisoned and tried. Late in 1861, he was convicted and sentenced to hang. Before his execution, however, he committed suicide in February 1862. This was the only case of a sea captain being sentenced to death for the slave trade. After this time, the participation of American ships in the international trade was virtually over.

The Internal Slave Trade

Inside the South, prices for slaves had greatly declined by the end of 1860. The possibility of war threatened the entire institution of slavery. As the war began, some internal slave trade continued. For example, traders carried slaves between Virginia and Alabama. Slave traders also continued to operate in South Carolina.

As Union armies invaded the South, however,

slave-trading routes were disrupted. Union ships also began blockading southern ports. In April 1862, a Union army captured New Orleans. Eventually, the slave pens and trading houses in the city were closed.

Slaves on the plantations reacted in many different ways. Some continued working as before. But others reduced the speed and quantity of their work. They heard that northern troops were approaching and believed they might soon be freed. Other slaves left the plantations to find the invading northern armies. In fact, an estimated five hundred thousand slaves fled or found protection behind the Union lines during the Civil War. One slave, Susie King, escaped from Savannah, Georgia, in 1862. As she recalled, "I wanted to see these wonderful 'Yankees' so much, as I heard my parents say the Yankee was going to set all the slaves free."[4]

Many slaves also served with the Union armies and fought against the Confederacy during the Civil War. Some enlisted as scouts. Their knowledge of southern roads helped guide federal forces as they invaded the South. They fought on battlefields across the Confederacy and helped free other slaves on the plantations.

These African Americans helped the North achieve a final victory in 1865. With the defeat of the South, the slave trade in the United States ended forever.

The Legacy of the Slave Trade

The slaves referred to them as "many thousands gone." They were slaves, sold from one plantation to another, who disappeared from their families. According to one estimate, more than 2 million slaves were sold as part of this internal slave trade.[5] This was over seven times the number of slaves imported from Africa.

In the internal trade, the slaves were taken from one state to another by traders who were called "soul drivers." The words of one slave song went:

> *William Rino sold Henry Silvers*
> *Hilo! Hilo!*
> *Sold him to de Georgy trader;*
> *Hilo! Hilo!*
> *His wife she cried, and children bawled,*
> *Hilo! Hilo!*
> *Sold him to de Georgy trader;*
> *Hilo! Hilo!*[6]

As historian Walter Johnson has pointed out, slaves were sold by their masters for a variety of reasons. They were sold to pay off debts, to punish them for not doing their work or because they ran away, or because they were "getting too proud and putting on 'white airs.'"[7] Planters used their power whenever it served their purposes. There was always a ready market for slaves. As the price of cotton continued to rise, planters wanted to cultivate more land. They needed more slaves to make bigger plantations profitable. As the demand grew, the prices continued to increase. Slaves were a good investment. The investment potential and the profit to be made on slaves continued to fuel the demand for them.

Large planters, however, were not the only ones who bought slaves. Throughout the South, the ownership of slaves was considered a mark of distinction. When someone could afford slaves, it meant that he or she had reached a certain position on the social scale. Many southerners wanted to achieve this position.[8] Slaves were also considered a sound investment for the future. As one young southerner put it: "For a young man just commencing in life the best stock in which he can invest capital is, I think, Negro stock [slaves]."[9]

For the slave traders, the constant flow of slaves provided them with a steady income. Some of these traders were large dealers who grew rich from the trade. Others were much smaller operators. But they all saw slave trading as a way of making money. Indeed, it accounted for a large part of the southern economy, putting money into the pockets not only of traders but planters, as well.

African Americans were oppressed by this trade. They were the people who died in the long voyages from Africa to America that began in the sixteenth

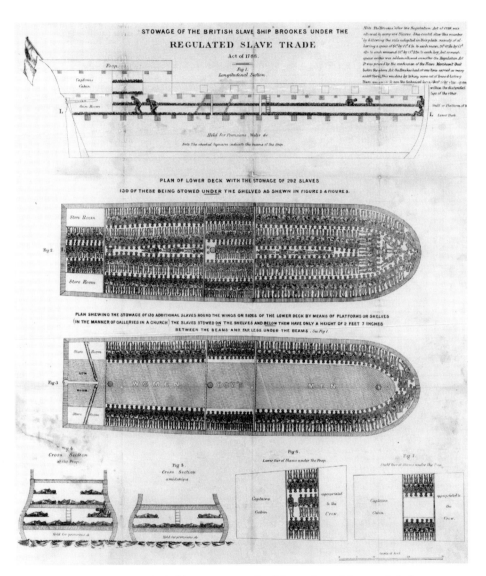

Men, women, and children were packed into slave ships as tightly as possible. These cramped conditions bred pain and disease.

SOURCE DOCUMENT

Sometimes a woman would have a child in her arms. A man would buy the mother and wouldn't want the child. And then sometimes a woman would holler out: "Don't sell that pickaninny." (You know they didn't call colored children nothin' but Pickaninnies then.) "I want that little pickaninny." And the mother would go one way and the child would go the other. The mother would be screaming and hollering, and of course, the child wouldn't be saying nothin' because it didn't know what was goin' on.[10]

H.B. Holloway, a former slave, describes the separation of mother and son on the auction block. Holloway was eighty-nine years old when he gave this interview in the late 1930s.

century and continued for more than three hundred years. They were the same people who might be sold again and again once they reached the plantations of the South. Once they were put on the auction blocks or the trading houses, these same slaves were expected to submit themselves to the humiliation of being sold like animals. As one slave put it,

When a Negro was put on the block he had to help sell himself by telling what he could do. If he refused to praise himself and acted sullen, he was sure to be stripped and given thirty lashes. Frequently a man was compelled to exaggerate his accomplishments, and when his buyer found out that he could not do what he said he could he would be beaten unmercifully. It was pretty sure a thrashing either way.[11]

However, slaves often resisted slavery and worked against it in various ways. They slowed their work, rebelled, and ran away. Some of those who escaped joined the abolition movement.

Only with an end to slavery and the slave trade in the 1860s did the harsh conditions of slavery come to an end. In 1863, President Lincoln issued the Emancipation Proclamation. This freed the slaves in the southern states fighting against the North. Meanwhile, African Americans were fleeing the plantations and joining the Union army. Slavery was later completely abolished as a result of the Thirteenth Amendment to the Constitution, ratified in 1865. African Americans who had helped bring about emancipation by resisting efforts of slavers to oppress them could now continue to chart a new destiny.

✦ T I M E L I N E ✦

1619	African workers arrive in North America, carried by a Dutch ship to the colony of Virginia.
1625	The first African slaves arrive in the Dutch colony of New Amsterdam (later called New York).
1672	The British establish the Royal African Company and give it a monopoly of African slave trade.
1720s	English merchants transport ten thousand slaves to North America.
1725	Newport, Rhode Island, enters the triangular trade.
1730s	British merchants transport forty thousand slaves to North America.
1787	The Constitutional Convention bans the importation of slaves by 1808.
1808	Legal importation of slaves in the United States ends.
1818	The United States passes a law giving informers rewards for exposing illegal slave traders.
1820	A United States law punishes illegal slave trade with death.
1839	The English ship *Buzzard* brings captured American slavers to New York. The *Amistad* is captured in New York.

1841	The United States Supreme Court decides the *Amistad* case.
1842	The Webster-Ashburton Treaty calls for American ships to patrol the African coast and stop illegal slave traders.
1850	The Compromise of 1850 stops internal slave trade in the District of Columbia.
1856	Rudolph Lasala is found not guilty of violating slave trade laws.
1858	A Charleston jury refuses to convict slave traders in the *Echo* case.
1859	The *Wanderer* illegally brings slaves to Savannah, Georgia.
1861	The Civil War begins. Nathaniel Gordon is convicted of slave trade and sentenced to death.
1863	Emancipation Proclamation frees the slaves in states of rebellion.
1865	Civil War ends. Thirteenth Amendment is passed, freeing all the slaves.

CHAPTER NOTES

CHAPTER 1. STORIES OF THE SLAVE TRADE

1. *Internet African History Sourcebook*, n.d. <http://vi.uh.edu/pages/mintz/4.htm> (July 7, 2003).

2. Ibid.

3. Ibid.

4. Ibid.

CHAPTER 2. ORIGINS OF THE SLAVE TRADE

1. Herbert S. Klein, *The Atlantic Slave Trade* (Cambridge, England: Cambridge University Press, 1999), pp. 3, 4.

2. Hugh Thomas, *The Slave Trade* (New York: Simon and Schuster, 1997), p. 34.

3. Klein, p. 6.

4. Thomas, p. 21.

5. Ibid., p. 69.

6. Ibid., p. 71.

7. Klein, p. 56.

8. "The Story of Africa: Central African Kingdoms," *BBC World Service*, n.d., <http://www.bbc.co.uk/worldservice/africa/features/storyofafrica/10chapter4.shtml> (August 26, 2003).

9. Thomas, p. 114.

10. *Oxford World Encyclopedia* (New York: Oxford University Press, 2001), p. 87.

11. Klein, p. 15.

12. Thomas, p. 136.

13. Ibid., p. 142.

CHAPTER 3. THE SLAVE TRADE IN THE 1600S

1. Hugh Thomas, *The Slave Trade* (New York: Simon and Schuster, 1997), pp. 62–64.

2. Ibid., p. 203.

3. David Eltis, *The Rise of African Slavery in the Americas* (Cambridge, England: Cambridge University Press, 2000), p. 48.

4. John Locke, "The Fundamental Constitutions of Carolina: March 1, 1669," *The Avalon Project at Yale Law School*, © 1998, <http://www.yale.edu/lawweb/avalon/states/nc05.htm> (August 26, 2003).

5. "John Locke," n.d., <http://www.english.nwu.edu/llipking/18thc/slavery/locke.html> (August 26, 2003).

6. Herbert S. Klein, *The Atlantic Slave Trade* (Cambridge, England: Cambridge University Press, 1999), p. 98.

7. Thomas, p. 443.

8. Klein, p. 83.

9. Thomas Howard, ed., *Black Voyage: Eyewitness Accounts of the Atlantic Slave Trade* (Boston: Little, Brown and Company, 1971), pp. 77, 78.

10. Daniel Mannix, *Black Cargoes: A History of the Atlantic Slave Trade, 1518–1865* (New York: Viking, 1962), p. 76.

11. Peter Kolchin, *American Slavery: 1619–1877* (New York: Hill and Wang, 1993), p. 21.

12. Klein, p. 150; Thomas, p. 423.

13. Howard, pp. 81, 85.

14. Ibid.

15. Klein, p. 83.

16. Howard, pp. 51, 52.

17. Ibid., p. 87.

18. Klein, p. 97.

19. Betty Wood, *The Origins of American Slavery* (New York: Hill and Wang, 1997), p. 88.

CHAPTER 4. THE SLAVE TRADE IN THE 1700S

1. Daniel Mannix, *Black Cargoes: A History of the Atlantic Slave Trade, 1518–1865* (New York: Viking, 1962), p. 160.

2. Jay Coughtry, "The Notorious Triangle," n.d. <http://www.cyberspace.org/~jh/wgh/coughtry.html> (September 8, 2003).

3. George Francis Dow, *Slave Ships and Slaving* (Port Washington, N.Y.: Kennikat Press, Inc., 1969), p. 259.

4. Hugh Thomas, *The Slave Trade* (New York: Simon and Schuster, 1997) p. 271.

5. Ira Berlin, *Many Thousands Gone: The First Two Centuries of Slavery in North America* (Cambridge, Mass.: Harvard University Press, 1998), p. 145.

6. Thomas, pp. 244, 246, 275.

7. Berlin, pp. 178–179.

8. Ibid., p. 146.

9. Ibid., p. 148.

10. Ibid., p. 303.

11. Frederic Bancroft, *Slave Trading in the Old South* (Columbia: University of South Carolina Press, 1996), p. 10.

12. Peter Kolchin, *American Slavery: 1619–1877* (New York: Hill and Wang, 1993), p. 95.

13. Ira Berlin, *Generations of Captivity: A History of African-American Slaves* (Cambridge, Mass.: Harvard University Press, 2003), p. 131.

CHAPTER 5. THE SLAVE TRADE AND THE LAW

1. Thomas Howard, ed., *Black Voyage: Eyewitness Accounts of the Atlantic Slave Trade* (Boston: Little, Brown, and Company 1971), pp. 130–131.

2. W.E.B. DuBois, *The Suppression of the African Slave-Trade to the United States of America, 1638–1870* (New York: Shocken Books, 1969), p. 95.

3. Herbert S. Klein, *The Atlantic Slave Trade* (Cambridge, England: Cambridge University Press, 1999), p. 199.

4. Warren S. Howard, *American Slavers and the Federal Law, 1837–1862* (Berkeley: University of California Press, 1963), p. 11.

5. DuBois, p. 110.

6. Hugh Thomas, *The Slave Trade* (New York: Simon and Schuster, 1997), p. 615.

7. Howard, p. 20.

8. Ibid., pp. 18–19.

9. DuBois, p. 147.

10. Howard, p. 144.

11. George Francis Dow, *Slave Ships and Slaving* (Port Washington, N.Y.: Kennikat Press, Inc., 1969), p. 277.

12. Michael Tadman, *Speculators and Slaves* (Madison: University of Wisconsin Press,1989), pp. 289–290.

CHAPTER 6. SLAVE TRADE WITHIN THE SOUTH

1. Ira Berlin, *Many Thousands Gone: The First Two Centuries of Slavery in America* (Cambridge, Mass.: Harvard University Press, 1998), p. 369.

2. Peter Kolchin, *American Slavery, 1619–1877* (New York: Hill and Wang, 1993), p. 93.

3. Berlin, p. 213.

4. Kolchin, p. 95.

5. Frederic Bancroft, *Slave Trading in the Old South* (Columbia: University of South Carolina Press, 1996), pp. 19, 25.

6. Ibid., p. 33.

7. Ira Berlin, *Generations of Captivity: A History of African-American Slaves* (Cambridge, Mass.: Harvard University Press, 2003), pp. 168–169.

8. Junius P. Rodriguez, ed., *The Historical Encyclopedia of World Slavery* (Santa Barbara, Calif.: ABC-CLIO, 1997), vol. 1, p. 220.

9. Michael Tadman, *Speculators and Slaves: Masters, Traders, and Slaves in the Old South* (Madison: University of Wisconsin Press, 1989), pp. 193–194.

10. Frederick Law Olmsted, *A Journey in the Seaboard Slave States* (New York: New American Library, 1969), p. 57.

11. Rodriguez, p. 100.

12. Tadman, p. 122.

13. Paul A. David, et al., *Reckoning With Slavery* (New York: Oxford University Press, 1976), p. 100.

14. Ibid., p. 129.

15. Rodriguez, p. 220.

16. Tadman, pp. 162–163.

17. Bancroft, p. 207.

18. Yuval Taylor, ed., *I Was Born a Slave: An Anthology of Classic Slave Narratives* (Chicago: Lawrence Hill Books), pp. 328–329.

19. Tadman, pp. 179–180.

20. Ibid.

21. "Laura Spicer: It Never Was Our Wish to Be Separated," n.d., <http://vi.uh.edu/pages/mintz/19.htm> (August 26, 2003).

22. Berlin, *Generations of Captivity*, pp. 172–174.

23. Olmsted, p. 55.

CHAPTER 7. MAJOR CENTERS OF THE INTERNAL SLAVE TRADE

1. Michael Tadman, *Speculators and Slaves: Masters, Traders, and Slaves in the Old South* (Madison: University of Wisconsin Press), p. 100.

2. Walter Johnson, *Soul by Soul: Life Inside the Antebellum Slave Market* (Cambridge, Mass.: Harvard University Press, 1999), pp. 48–49.

3. Ira Berlin, *Generations of Captivity: A History of African-American Slaves* (Cambridge, Mass.: Harvard University Press, 2003), p. 180.

4. Yuval Taylor, ed., *I Was Born a Slave: An Anthology of Classic Slave Narratives, Vol. 2* (Chicago: Lawrence Hill Books, 1999), pp. 362–363.

5. Ibid.

6. Ibid.

7. Ibid.

8. Johnson, p. 45.

9. American Slave Narratives, August 10, 1997, <http://xroads.virginia.edu/~hyper/wpa/holmes1.html> (July 7, 2003).

10. Eyre Crowe, "In the Richmond Slave Market," *History Matters*, n.d., <http://historymatters.gmu.edu/d/6762> (August 26, 2003).

11. Frederic Bancroft, *Slave Trading In The Old South* (Columbia: University of South Carolina Press, 1996), p. 303.

12. Michael Trinkley, "Buying and Selling Human Beings: The Price of a Human Being," *SCIway*, © 2003, <http://sciway.net/afam/slavery/flesh.html> (September 8, 2003).

13. Tadman, p. 62.

14. Ibid., p. 58.

15. Bancroft, pp. 115–116.

16. Taylor, pp. 182–184.

17. Ibid.

18. Ibid.

19. Tadman, p. 290.

20. Johnson, p. 23.

21. Ibid., p. 22.

22. American Slave Narratives, August 10, 1997, <http://xroads.virginia.edu/~hyper/wpa/hughes1.html> (July 7, 2003).

23. Tadman, p. 131.

CHAPTER 8. END OF THE SLAVE TRADE

1. Thomas Howard, ed., *Black Voyage: Eyewitness Accounts of the Atlantic Slave Trade* (Boston: Little, Brown, and Company 1971), pp. 163–164.

2. W.E.B. DuBois, *The Suppression of the African Slave-Trade to the United States of America, 1638–1870* (New York: Schocken Books, 1969), p. 189.

3. Daniel Mannix, *Black Cargoes: A History of the Atlantic Slave Trade, 1518–1865* (New York: Viking Press, 1962), p. 273.

4. James M. McPherson, *The Negro's Civil War* (New York: Random House, 1965), pp. 56–57.

5. Walter Johnson, *Soul By Soul: Life Inside the Antebellum Slave Market* (Cambridge, Mass.: Harvard University Press, 1999), p. 7.

6. Ibid., p. 43.

7. Ibid., pp. 27–28.

8. Ibid., p. 82.

9. Ibid., p. 83.

10. "Ex-Slave: Slave Sales," *Born in Slavery: Slave Narratives From the Federal Writers' Project*, n.d., <http://memory.loc.gov/cgi-bin/ampage?collId=mesn&fileName=023/mesn023.db&recNum=289&tempFile=./temp/~ammem_8604&filecode=mesn&next_filecode=mesn&prev_filecode=mesn&itemnum=2&ndocs=100> (August 26, 2003).

11. Johnson, p. 177.

BARRACOON—Large quarters in Africa where slaves were imprisoned before shipment to the New World.

BLACK DEATH—A plague, carried to humans by fleas that lived on rats, that first struck Europe during the late Middle Ages.

COFFLES—Long lines of slaves roped together for transport through the South.

EMANCIPATION PROCLAMATION—Issued by President Abraham Lincoln in 1863, this document freed slaves in the southern states fighting against the North.

ENCOMIENDAS—Huge estates given to Spanish settlers in the New World.

INDENTURED SERVANTS—Workers who agreed to serve planters in the New World for a specified period of time to work off their debts.

INDIGO—A blue dye used to color fabrics.

MIDDLE PASSAGE—The transatlantic voyage of slaves from Africa to the New World.

PLANTATION—Large farm for growing crops such as sugarcane, rice, and cotton.

SLAVE COAST—The west coast of Africa from the Volta to the Niger rivers.

TRIANGULAR TRADE—Rum from Rhode Island shipped to Africa and traded for slaves, who were brought to the West Indies and sold for sugar and molasses, which was then taken to Rhode Island to make rum.

FURTHER READING

Altman, Linda Jacobs. *Slavery and Abolition in American History*. Berkeley Heights, N.J.: Enslow Publishers, Inc., 1999.

Currie, Stephen. *Life of a Slave on a Southern Plantation*. San Diego: Lucent Books, 2000.

Haskins, James, and Kathleen Benson. *Bound for America: The Forced Migration of Africans to the New World*. New York: Lothrop, Lee & Shepard Books, 1999.

Lester, Julius. *To Be a Slave*. New York: Dial Books, 1998.

Meltzer, Milton. *They Came in Chains: The Story of the Slave Ships*. New York: Benchmark Books, 2000.

Palmer, Colin A. *The First Passage: Blacks in the Americas, 1502–1617*. New York: The Oxford University Press, 1995.

Paulson, Timothy. *Days of Sorrow, Years of Glory 1813–1850: From the Nat Turner Revolt to the Fugitive Slave Law*. Philadelphia: Chelsea House, 1994.

Zeinert, Karen. *The* Amistad *Slave Revolt and American Abolition*. North Haven, Conn.: Shoe String Press, Inc., 1997.

✦ Internet ✦ Addresses

Handler, Jerome S. and Michael L. Tuite Jr. "The Atlantic Slave Trade and Slave Life in the Americas: A Visual Record." *The University of Virginia Library.* n. d. <http://hitchcock.itc.virginia.edu/Slavery/>.

Internet Modern History Sourcebook. © 1997 <http://www.fordham.edu/halsall/mod/modsbook.html>.

Linder, Doug. "Amistad Trials: 1839–1840." *Famous Trials.* © 1998. <http://www.law.umkc.edu/faculty/projects/ftrials/amistad/AMISTD.HTM>.

✦ Historic ✦ Sites

Anacostia Museum & Center for African-American History and Culture
1901 Fort Pl., SE, Washington, D.C.
(202) 287-3306
http://anacostia.si.edu
JCTolson@am.si.edu

Slave Mart Museum
6 Chalmers St., Charleston, S.C. 29401
(843) 724-7395

A

Adams, John Quincy, 68–69
Affonso I, 18
Africa, 7, 8, 10, 12, 13, 14, 15,
    16–19, 21–22, 23, 25, 26, 27,
    28, 31, 34–35, 38, 40, 43, 44,
    47, 48, 49, 50, 55, 60–61, 62,
    63–64, 65, 66, 68, 69, 70, 72,
    73, 78, 87, 104, 105, 106,
    107, 108, 109, 112, 113
Alabama, 57, 63, 72, 73, 74, 77,
    78, 79, 88, 95, 107
American Revolution, 52, 54, 55,
    76
Amistad, 66, 68
Andrews, Ethan, 84
Arkansas, 73, 78, 82
Aztec empire, 22

B

Barbados, 30, 31, 32, 33, 34
Beard, Joseph A. 93
Berlin, Ira, 51, 77
Betts, Samuel R., 70
Black Death, 23
B. M. Campbell, 79
Brazil, 22, 28, 60, 70
Brown, John, 91–92
Brown, William, 89
Bryan, Joseph, 96–97
Burch, James H., 99, 100
Buzzard, 65

C

California, 100
Caribbean Indians, 20–21, 30
Central Park, 81
Charlemagne, 12

Charles I, 31
Charles II, 31
Chile, 22
China, 20
Cinqué, 68
Civil War, 103, 108
Columbus, Christopher, 19–20
Compromise of 1850, 100, 101
Confederate States of America,
    106, 108
Connecticut, 47, 54, 56, 104
Constitution, 113
Constitutional Convention, 65
Cortes, Hernán, 22
Cromwell, Oliver, 31
Cuba, 21, 22, 61, 66, 68, 70, 105
Curaçao, 28

D

Decatur, 78
Declaration of Independence, 52
Delaware, 82
de Sweerts, Jan, 28
DuBois, W.E.B., 69
Dukandara people, 7

E

East Florida, 48
Echo, 70
Ecuador, 22
Emancipation Proclamation, 113
England, 23, 26, 27, 28, 30–31,
    32–33, 34, 40, 42, 46, 49, 51,
    52, 54, 55, 58, 59–61, 62, 63,
    65, 69, 74, 76, 106
Erie, 107

F

Falconbridge, Alexander, 8, 10, 58

Ferdinand, 20
Filmore, Millard, 100
Florida, 51, 63, 73, 74
France, 12, 23, 27, 30, 46, 51, 56, 74
Franklin & Armfield, 79, 90

G

Gadsden, Thomas, 80
Gauls, 11
Georgia, 48, 50, 51, 52, 54, 55, 57, 71–72, 88, 96, 97, 108
Germany, 11–12
Gideon, 28
Gordon, Nathaniel, 107
Guinea, 7

H

Hagan, John, 90
Hannibal, 40, 41, 42
Henry, Prince of Portugal, 14
Hispaniola, 20, 21
Holmes, Joseph, 95
Howard, Warren, 70
Hughes, Fountain, 102
Hungary, 13

I

Incas, 22
India, 17, 20
Isabella, Queen, 20
Islam, 12
Italy, 11, 13, 20

J

Jamaica, 32
Jamestown, 27
Jefferson, Thomas, 59, 74, 76
John I, 14
Johnson, George, 102
Johnson, Walter, 109
J. W. Neal & Company, 99

K

Kentucky, 95, 106
King Solomon, 28
King, Susie, 108
Klein, Herbert, 13, 23
Kolchin, Peter, 38

L

Lafitte, Jean, 62
Lasala, Rudolph E., 70
Laurens, Henry, 48
Le Louis, 59
Lincoln, Abraham, 105–106, 113
Louisiana, 51–52, 57, 62, 63, 73, 74, 78, 79, 82, 87, 88, 89, 90, 93, 94, 95, 98, 99, 105, 108
Louisiana Purchase, 74
Lopez, Aaron, 44
Lumpkin, Bob, 97

M

Madison, James, 61–62
Manning, Edward, 104–105
Mannix, Daniel, 37
Maryland, 32, 43, 50, 55, 73, 76, 77, 78, 82, 87, 99
Massachusetts, 32, 47, 52, 69, 74
Matthews, Branton & Company, 79
Mexican War, 100
Mexico, 22, 62, 100, 105
Middle Passage, 38, 40–41, 44, 46
Mississippi, 57, 72, 73, 74, 77, 78, 79, 82, 87, 95
Mississippi River, 87, 89, 95
Missouri, 106
Monroe, James, 63
Muhammad, 12
Mumford, Robert, 7
Muslims, 12–14

N

Netherlands, 23, 27–28, 31

Neville, Julian, 93
New Amsterdam. *See* New York.
New Hampshire, 52
New Mexico, 100
New York, 28, 48, 52, 62, 63, 65, 66, 68, 81
North Carolina, 32, 50, 57, 78, 82, 95
Northrup, Solomon, 99–100

O
Olmsted, Frederick Law, 81, 88

P
Pennsylvania, 54
Peru, 22
Philip II, 23, 26
Phillips, Thomas, 40
Pieterson, Dirck, 28
Pizarro, Francisco, 22
Portugal, 14, 15–19, 22, 23, 27, 28, 44, 60, 62
Puerto Rico, 21
Puritans, 31

R
Rhode Island, 7, 44, 46, 48, 54, 56
Rome, 11
Royal African Company, 31–32, 35, 36
Russia, 13

S
St. Charles Hotel, 93
St. John, 28
St. Kitts, 30, 33
St. Louis Hotel, 93
Santo Domingo, 56
Saudi Arabia, 12
Second Middle Passage, 77
Smith, Venture, 7
South America, 61, 65

South Carolina, 32, 48, 50–51, 54, 55, 57, 70, 76, 78, 80, 82, 87, 88, 90, 95, 96, 107
Spain, 12, 13–14, 19–22, 23, 26, 27, 28, 48, 51, 60–61, 62, 63, 64, 65, 66, 68, 74
Spectators and Slaves, 79
Supreme Court, 68, 69

T
Tadman, Michael, 79, 81–82, 83, 85
Tallmadge, James, 63
Tennessee, 72, 87
Texas, 62, 73, 74, 78, 82
Thomas A. Powell & Company, 79
Thomas, Hugh, 22, 25
Thomas Watson, 104–105
Thirteenth Amendment, 113

U
United States Congress, 59, 63, 107
United States Senate, 100
Utah, 100

V
Van Buren, Martin, 68
Venus, 51–52
Virginia, 27, 32, 43, 50, 55, 73, 76, 77, 78, 79, 81, 82, 87, 88, 90, 95, 97, 99, 101, 107

W
Wanderer, 71
Washington, D.C., 99–100
Webster-Ashburton Treaty, 69
West India Company, 28
West Indies, 44, 45, 47, 48, 55
White, John, 94
Whitney, Eli, 56
Woolfolk, Austin, 78

Y
Yeamans, John, 32